MW00619907

The Candle Magick
WORKBOOK

The Candle Magick
WORKBOOK

By Kala and Ketz Pajeon

𝑘

Citadel Press
Kensington Publishing Corp.
www.kensingtonbooks.com

CITADEL PRESS books are published by

Kensington Publishing Corp.
850 Third Avenue
New York, NY 10022

All Kensington titles, imprints, and distributed lines are available at special quantity discounts for bulk purchases for sales promotions, premiums, fund raising, educational, or institutional use. Special book excerpts or customized printings can also be created to fit specific needs. For details, write or phone the office of the Kensington special sales manager: Kensington Publishing Corp., 850 Third Avenue, New York, NY 10022, attn: Special Sales Department, phone 1-800-221-2647.

Kensington and the K logo Reg. U.S. Pat. & TM Office
Citadel Press is a trademark of Kensington Publishing Corp.

First printing 1991

19 18 17 16 15 14 13 12 11

Printed in the United States of America

Library of Congress Cataloging-in-Publication Data

Pajeon, Kala.
    The candle magick workbook / by Kala and Ketz Pajeon.
        p.   cm.
    "A Citadel Press Book."
    ISBN 0-8065-1268-7 (pbk.)
    1. Magic.   2. Candles—Miscelleana.   I. Pajeon, Ketz   II. Title.
BF1623.C26P25   1991
133.4'3—dc20   91-30767
                                        CIP

To the Old and Ancient Ones
and the Lady in Blue

ARTIST INFORMATION

Contributing Artist

Carol Law
c/o Kala Pajeon
47000 Warms Springs Blvd. Suite 302
Fremont, California 94539

Graphic Design
Created by Kala Pajeon using Computer Clip Art from:

Wet Paint Series Clip Art by Double Click
9316 Deering Avenue
Chattsworth, California   91311

Enzan-Hoshigumi Co., Ltd.
Suite 805, Harajuku Green Height
53-17, Sendagaya 3 Chrome
Shibuya-ku, Tokyo, 151 Japan
(Scroll 1: "Heaven," Premaevus File/item #20 Deer and
Hunter Bronze Age)

The authors wish to give special thanks to June G. Bletzer, Ph.D., and The Donning Press for allowing us to quote extensively from their book *The Donning International Encyclopedic Psychic Dictionary.*

Contents

PART SIX

PART SEVEN

PART EIGHT

PART NINE

Acknowledgments

We wish to express our heartfelt appreciation to the following for their most valuable assistance and encouragement.

Mary Greer, a truly unselfish friend who helped Kala to remember. San Jose Book Store, Shirley, Jan, Heather, and Alondria, the chapter on "Ethics" is dedicated to you. Mary Kittridge, *Writer's Digest*. Meera Lester, *Writer's Connection*. Finally, my students, particularly Shelly, Cynthia, Phyllis and Sharon for their input and support.

Goals of a Natural Magickian*

1. To walk in harmony with nature, never taking without giving.
2. To understand that magick is an alliance between humans and the Earth for the betterment of all.
3. To use magic as an instrument of loving change, not hateful destruction.
4. To see the spiritual in the physical and to understand that neither is higher nor more perfect than the other.
5. To wisely use natural energies only when in genuine need, not for greed.
6. To know that nothing is impossible if we will work beyond personal limitations.
7. To work magic for others only with their permission.
8. To celebrate magic as a union with the energies that gave us our physical forms.
9. To improve ourselves, our friends and our world for the greater good of all.

*Reprinted with permission from Llewellyn Publications, ''The Magickal Almanac,'' page 233 and quoted from Scott Cunningham.

Preface

WHAT THIS WORKBOOK CAN DO FOR YOU

There are many systems of magick in the world today and there are hundreds of books on the market dealing with each system. You will find extensive works on High Magick, Low Magick, Rune Magick, and Talisman Magick. Yet very little can be found concerning one of the oldest and most potent systems of magick in human history, Candle Magick.

This being the case as we have found it, we have created, by illustrating our own personal methods, what we believe to be the most thorough and comprehensive workbook on generic Candle Magick available today.

Our workbook serves a twofold purpose. It (1) serves as a springboard to other systems of magick by teaching the why and how of magick in an easy, step-by-step process, thus offering rapid growth potential, and (2) begins where other works on the subject leave off.

Too often ignored is why and how Candle Magick works. This is covered in the workbook to ensure success and avoid pitfalls.

If you have recently searched for a good reference text on Candle Magick, you know how little is available to choose from. If by chance you succeed in locating a text that does not just mention Candle Magick in passing or relegates it to a secondary topic, that text rarely tells you everything you need or want to know. You mostly wind up with a book of recipes. Too often the text leaves the reader with many unanswered questions:

- Why is Candle Magick effective in obtaining love, money, health, protection, and promotions?
- How can you rid yourself of unwanted suitors, nosy busybodies, or ex-lovers?

- What effects can Candle Magick have on you and others by its use or misuse?
- How can you obtain the same or better results each time you use Candle Magick?
- How can Candle Magick help develop your own ESP?
- How can you interpret the language of the burning candle, read its smoke, or analyze its flame?

This workbook was produced for the serious student of Candle Magick. It is presented in generic form and will give you a sound basis from which to build.

As there are many methods of Candle Magick ranging from the simple making of a wish and blowing out of a candle, to the more complex devotions to the Saints, confusion is easy and mistakes are costly.

To avoid the mistakes and confusion new practitioners often encounter, a step-by-step worksheet will guide you throughout the entire Candle Magick process. This special guidance builds confidence and promotes rapid growth to more complex methods of magick.

Finally, what are your responsibilities and possible karmic repercussions when practicing magick? Knowing how to get what you want without producing negative karma is the mark of a true master.

As will be demonstrated, Candle Magick is not a superstition. It is an actual working philosophy of life, as is all magick. Should you have doubts as to its reality or effectiveness, we offer this workbook as evidence. The same techniques we use in our lives we share with you throughout this workbook.

Foreword

*"I call upon Vesta, Keeper of the Sacred Flame, to bring
blessings on this book and on its makers."*

In Greece, all ceremonies and new enterprises began with an
offering to the altar of Hestia, as Vesta was then known. I ask
Vesta as Goddess of the hospitality of the hearth to welcome
you to this work. Within Vesta's sanctuary of protection may
you safely explore her ancient, magickal, ever-renewing fire.
Before her hearth, upon your altar, may your goals find their
point of focus, intensify, and then be released to manifest in
the world for your greatest good and that of All Creation.

In *The Candle Magick Workbook*, Kala and Ketz Pajeon have
brought together everything you need to make Candle Magick
a powerful and effective way of manifesting your desires.
Their expertise is a gift shared with love.

Although you may find other books telling you which color
candle and which oil to use for any purpose, it is only in this
book that you will find the deeper secrets of preparing yourself to work Candle Magick with clarity and inner trust, from
a place where you are united with all parts of yourself.
Remember that all magick returns to you threefold, and so use
the tools you find within, as well as without, to make this
world and your life a brighter place. Just as Vesta's hearth was
in the center of all dwellings, so too is the light of each candle
you burn in magick at the center of your earthly dwelling—in
your heart. As Cicero said, the flame of Vesta is "the guardian of all innermost things." May you find in the outer flame

a mirror image of the flame within, and by its light find your way to the unique expression of the joyous being you are. Vesta's children, Kala and Ketz, have been gifted and entrusted with her sacred teachings, and are now your guides into the realm of candle magick. I leave you to their care.

Blessed Be,
Mary K. Greer
Nevada City, California
January 1991
(author of *Tarot for Your Self:*
A Workbook for Personal Transformation)

The Candle Magick
WORKBOOK

PART ONE

Man is but a reed, the most weak in Nature, but he is a
thinking reed.

—Blaise Pascal (1623–1662)

1

History of Fire and Candle Magick

A Workbook on Candle Magick would not be complete without a brief history of the discovery and cultivation of fire. One would believe that an element that has been with the human species for so long would be easy to trace. Due primarily to a lack of written records, fire is shrouded in mystery. Its exact time and method of discovery as well as to how and when it was first cultivated for human use is unknown.

With unnerving frequency, anthropologists are unearthing new evidence that continually sets back the clock for not only the discovery and use of fire, but the history of our human species as well, thus making exact dates impossible to discern.

Anthropologists have suggested that the discovery of fire not only has led to our current civilization, but fire has set humans apart from other species.

It is currently believed that fire was first collected from natural sources approximately 250,000 to 500,000 years ago.

The first human kindling of fire occurred approximately 50,000 years ago while true domestication of fire occurred as late as 10,000 years ago, according to the *Encyclopedia of Religion*, Vol. 5, 1987.

To demonstrate some of the controversy over the historical time line of fire, we include an excerpt from the *Reader's Digest Book of Facts* dated 1987. "The human line, the hominids, has known how to use fire for at least 500,000 years and has probably been able to make fire since about 12,000 years ago." While the *Chronicle of the World*, 1989, states, "China, c. 350,000 B.C. The caves of Zhoukoudian (Dragon Bone Hill), north of the Yellow River in northeast China, have been occupied by *Homo erectus* for 100,000 years. These humans seem to have mastered the use of fire."

Some schools of thought believe that nature provided our early ancestors with their first awareness of fire when vegetation burned as a result of lightning storms, volcanic activity, or other natural means. Without the knowledge or means to start their own fires, hot coals or embers had to be carried from place to place in order to ensure that there was always a fire for immediate use.

Later, in the natural progression of our species, fire production by human hands was believed to have been discovered by accident. Most probably this "accident" occurred when someone in the process of shaping a flint tool observed a spark fall into some dry leaves, with obvious results. Other "accidents" might have occurred when the sun's rays were magnified through a piece of natural glass or someone sat around and patiently rubbed two sticks together. Whatever the cause, humans soon found that they did not have to carry around that burning coal or ember wherever they went.

Apart from the "natural" discovery of fire, early legends state that fire was either stolen from or was a gift from the reigning Gods and Goddesses of the time.

According to legend, Prometheus, the Son of the Titan Iapetus, had sympathy for humans and their sufferings. He, therefore, stole fire from heaven and brought it to Earth for human use.

As many of the early Gods and Goddesses were fire deities, said to control volcanoes, lightning, etc., the taking of fire from one of these sources would have been considered theft without the proper appeasement ritual.

One belief nearly every culture seems to agree with is that fire represents the ultimate power and ability to purify. It represents spirit in its purest form, the manifestation of God or Goddess and the vehicle by which to reach them.

The sacred or holy fires (gifts of the God or Goddess and not made by human hands) gave way to portable fires such as the torch, oil lamp, and candle. For convenience, the candle became the most popular method by which to communicate with the higher aspects of self and the God or Goddess source. Its flame represented the spirit's highest potential, while the smoke carried the prayers and desires to the deities. Herbal offerings placed in the flames or embodied within the candle itself gave off a pleasing scent that often induced an hypnotic state of awareness. This altered state of consciousness, whether induced by flame, prayer, chant, song, dance, herb, or any combination thereof, and accompanied by strong desire, created a mysterious response called magick.

Eventually it was found that properly manufactured candles encompassed all the essential elements, necessary to produce this magickal state, in one compact unit. The candle's popularity as one of the ultimate magickal tools was assured.

Not until the advent of electricity did the candle come into jeopardy as a tool of light, magick, and religious petition.

In contemporary religious observances, candle usage has declined in favor of more modern, less costly, and less dangerous devices that completely negate the reasons that candles were employed in the first place. As Michael Mack points out in his article in *U.S. Catholic* published in April 1989, "For a variety of reasons many Catholic Churches have replaced the traditional wax candles with electric lights..." The author goes on to note that many of the parishioners have objected to this and a large portion of the churches still keep the votive candles on hand. He adds, though, that, due to the fire hazard, all flames are extinguished at night when unattended. While this is probably a sound safety practice as far as the everyday world is concerned, it is highly questionable when it comes to prayer and magick.

Modern mundane thinking notwithstanding, the use of the

candle and flame in rituals of prayer and magick still persists. What is it that keeps people coming back to this ancient belief? Could it be that the flame touches something deep within our being that connects us to the Infinite, our magickal roots? Could there really be something to the legends of magick and its accompanying folklore?

These are questions only you, the practitioner of magick, can answer for yourself as you rediscover the magick of candles and what this magick can do for you and your life.

2

Forgotten Magick

We can still find Candle Magick hidden in many of our holiday and cultural celebrations. For example:

All Hollows or Samhain: This is the one night of the year when the thin veil between the living and the dead can easily be breached and divination is best. Many Latin American cultures still keep with the custom of preparing an altar on this night and placing upon it a picture of the departed loved ones. Candles, representing the spirits of the dead, are also placed upon the altar along with various symbols of death. Symbols of life represented by food, clothing, and tools are then added in hope that the departed will return to visit those left behind.

Over the years, this ceremony of love has been perverted into a ceremony of fear, now known colloquially as Halloween. Candles are placed in grotesque jack-o'-lanterns to ward off evil and keep away the dead. The ugly faces on pumpkins and masks are designed to frighten away such ''evils'' as ghosts, demons, goblins, and ghouls. The roots of this loving-turned-fearful ceremony are often lost on the children, dressed in scary costumes, going door to door for treats.

Birthdays: Many cultures made use of a tall candle marked

in twenty-one segments. The candle, purchased and blessed on the birthday of the child, was then lit on each consecutive birthday until the child reached maturity at age twenty-one. The burning of the candle on each birthday represented the gratitude of the child and family to a deity for that past year of life and also petitioned for many prosperous and healthful years to come.

The magickal and religious aspects of this candle burning have for the most part been lost and replaced with the small candles atop the birthday cake. The honoree is then told to "make a wish" which will come true if all candles are extinguished with one blow. The participants probably never realize they are indulging in Candle Magick.

Candlewalk: According to *The Folklore of American Holidays*, 1987, a remnant of the ancient midwinter fire festival appears today, celebrated regularly on Christmas Eve and New Year's Eve by the black people of rural Bladen County in North Carolina.

On this festive occasion, women and children disappear into a secret place, each adult carrying a torch or candle, while men must stay behind. Usually the men wait in a nearby church as it is rumored the penalty for following the women can be death.

Later, the women and children return, walking in a single file toward the church. Upon their entering, each torch and candle is extinguished.

This Candlewalk ritual—still a very secret rite about which little is actually known—is believed to be a form of worship of the Virgin Mary. It possibly consists of a celebration of the rite of passage of children into puberty.

Devotion Candles: These are usually taper, votive, novena, or oil candles that are offered to a particular Saint, Deity, or Loa for their help. Pagans, Catholics, and some Protestants, along with devotees of many African-based religions, still remember the value of a candle in ritual, magick, and prayer.

Drawing Down the Sun: In order to obtain a flame that was untouched or uncontaminated by mortals, ancient magickians and priests often used a piece of natural glass that would concentrate and magnify the Sun's rays. The rays were directed onto some dried grass, herbs, or holy resins. Once heated, the fuel would ignite into a flame to kindle the holy fires. Thus the fire was indeed sacred, as it was kindled by the deity.

Funerals: Candle or Fire Magick has played a significant role in funeral services of all cultures since the dawn of civilization. Funeral pyres cremated the physical remains. Torches and candles lined the processional paths to guide the spirit to the final resting place. Ancestors were guided across the threshold of death by song, dance, and fire.

Today, for some whom the funeral ritual has lost much of its spiritual significance, modern crematoriums and electric lights have replaced the open fire and candle. Many, though, still make use of the flame, in some form, to light the way for the departed.

Hanukkah: The Feast of Lights. This is an eight-day Jewish victory celebration commemorating the defeat of King Antiochus IV, who had sent troops to Judea to destroy the Jewish religion. It also commemorates the rededication of the temple and the relighting of the perpetual fire. Candles are lit for eight consecutive nights to celebrate this festive occasion.

Imbolg: A celebration of the Fire Goddess Brigid, also known as Brid, Bride, Bright, Bridgit, Brigit. The word Imbolg means "New Lambs" or "In the Womb." Imbolg signals the beginning of Spring and the birth of new life. It is also called the Feast of Lights or the Feast of Pan.

The Spirit of the House: When a household has known much happiness and prosperity, there is an old belief that the house has a good spirit. You can invite this spirit to accompany you when you move by taking the flame from the fireplace and using it to light a large candle. You then carry the lit candle to the new house and use it to start the new hearth fire.

Vernal Equinox: The time each year when all sacred or perpetual fires were extinguished. Holy men and women would relight the sacred flames in a ritual rededication. Members of the community then took home with them a spark of the Deity to relight their own hearth fires. This ritual was believed to bring prosperity and protection for the coming year to all who participated and demonstrated dedication to the Deity.

Vigilance Candles: Vigilance candles are used to create unity and change. Lit candles, each held by an individual, channel the masses' spiritual energy toward the desired goal. A lone vigilance candle, usually placed in a window or upon an altar, is used to guide the return or manifest the protection of a loved one on a journey.

Yule: The Yule celebration of rebirth, symbolized by the coming of the Sun and warmth once again to a cold environment on the longest night and shortest day of the year, predates Christianity. The Goddess, pregnant with life, the embodiment of regeneration, reincarnation, the renewal of all life, gives birth to the Sun.

With the advent of Christianity, the pagan rituals gave way to the religious aspect of the SON rather than the SUN being celebrated at Yule.

Whatever the reason for celebrating the Yule, all those participating used candles to signify rebirth. From the pagan altar candles to the Yule log fire and the Christmas tree lights, the spirit of birth and rebirth remains prevalent over the Yule season.

There are hundreds of similar examples of man's use and worship of fire. Taking an overall look at the way fire has been used as a tool, one can readily see that Candle Magick has been **an intricate** part of our lives.

HISTORY AND FORGOTTEN MAGICK

MIXED QUIZ

1. When was fire first discovered?
2. When was fire first collected by early humans?
3. Who was Prometheus?
4. One belief about fire held to common belief is that fire represents the ultimate power and ability to purify. (True or False)
5. A properly made candle contains all elements necessary to create an altered state of awareness. (True or False)

FOR YOUR NOTES

TEST YOUR KNOWLEDGE

ANSWER SHEET

1. The actual date for the discovery of fire is unknown.
2. The exact date is unknown. Researchers speculate the time frame to be between 250,000 and 500,000 years ago.
3. The son of the Titan God, Iapetus, in Greek legend.
4. True
5. True

3

The Lost Art of Candle Magick

Today, while most magickal systems encompass the use of candles in their rituals, candles are usually relegated to a passive role. Few practitioners know the real potential of the candle and fewer still recognize its use as a system of magick.

Many magickal and religious systems still incorporate candles into their practices but most have forgotten or now ignore the magickal roots of fire. This omission, for whatever reason, greatly reduces the effectiveness of the candle as a magickal tool or petition conveyance.

Throughout history, candles and Candle Magick have been so much a part of our lives it would be a shame to lose them to modern innovations, particularly when those innovations will not improve on the original but are merely used as cost saving or supposed safety measures.

In hopes of deterring this trend to modernize the old ways, we have written our account of Candle Magick so that others might build upon our endeavors. (Since Candle Magick is all that remains of an even earlier form of Fire Magick practiced by our ancestors, the terms fire and flame are used interchangeably throughout this workbook).

Candle Magick, like any other system of magick, can be made as simple or elaborate as one wishes. If you prefer the rigors of a challenge, Candle Magick can offer you this or it can offer you the simplicity of merely lighting a dedicated candle. Long complicated rituals and strange languages are not necessary here and often the simplest Candle Magick can give the same results.

In one of the editorial columns of a popular magazine dealing with magick, we recently read that a magickian had extolled the virtues of a particular form of High Ritual Magick. He first lamented about the challenges he had faced and then enthused about the final rewarding outcome.

In response, another individual, obviously unimpressed, asked the editor why people should be willing to go through such rigors when simple Candle Magick could produce the same results with much less ''hassle.''

Do not get us wrong here. We enjoy and practice Ritual Magick along with several other forms of magick. We do not believe one superior to another as far as results go. However, we must confess it tickled us to find someone else who knew our secret. Candle Magick is a potent system that is also one of the easiest to perform. Using far less regalia, one can perform it in the home right under unsuspecting eyes.

Should you be fortunate enough to have a secluded place, away from prying eyes, then ritual regalia is fun and helps to set the psychic magickal mood. If this luxury is not the case, Candle Magick should be your definite choice.

For example, dinners by candlelight are romantic and can be utilized as an aid to your magickal goal. No one needs to know you are serving magick along with the wine.

In your home, why not burn candles for their fragrance and to cover odors caused by pipes, cigarettes, pets, cooking, and general stuffiness? Of course you needn't tell visitors the candle is actually to neutralize his or her vexatious energy in your otherwise pleasant home. Do you actually believe that anyone would suspect your intentions were for anything but decoration or atmosphere? Not at all.

Candles, coming in a variety of shapes, sizes and colors, look wonderfully innocent and nondescript. A magickal candle does not have to be of a specialty variety such as black cats, mummies, crosses, or human figures. Although it is appropriate to use such candles when necessary, the standard taper or votive may be substituted when in the "public" view. We cover this more in detail in the chapter entitled "Exclusively Candles."

Candle Magick will not solve all your problems immediately nor will it change the world overnight, but it is a powerful tool toward those ends. It can also help you to realize that events can be altered and influenced by the will. Candle Magick further demonstrates that we are not helpless bystanders or victims, and we can take appropriate action to alter our reality. For that very reason, magick has been feared throughout the ages.

As an example, during the Second World War, Hitler was planning to invade England. Why did Hitler suddenly stop his Luftwaffe during the Battle of Britain with victory perhaps at hand?

There is a belief among the Wiccans that when the witches of England found out about Hitler's plan to invade, they banned together and used their combined powers to turn him away. No one, of course, understood why Hitler suddenly abandoned his plans at the very last moment. It is rumored that right up to the very night before the Luftwaffe was decimated, the witches of England were at work. The rest, as they say, is history.

TEST YOUR KNOWLEDGE

THE LOST ART OF CANDLE MAGICK

TRUE OR FALSE

1. Candle Magick can be as simple or as complex as you want it to be.
2. Candles come in a variety of shapes, sizes and colors, all of which can be used in Candle Magick.

3. Candle Magick can solve all your problems overnight.
4. As an individual, you are helpless to alter your reality and that of the world around you.
5. The Candle Magick Workbook describes a method of magick that teaches you how to alter your own reality and that of the world around you.

FOR YOUR NOTES

TEST YOUR KNOWLEDGE

ANSWER SHEET

1. True
2. True
3. False—Candle Magick will not solve all your problems immediately or will it change the world overnight, but it is a powerful tool for you to employ in this endeavor.
4. False—You do have the power to alter reality and the world around you, as taught in this workbook.
5. True

PART TWO

The tragedy and the magnificence of *Homo sapiens* together rise from the same smokey truth that we alone among the animal species refuse to acknowledge natural law.

—Robert Ardrey (1908–1980)

1

The Laws of Cause and Effect

ENERGY

We live in a sea of living energy that is in constant motion.

According to Dr. June G. Bletzer, in *The Donning International Encyclopedic Psychic Dictionary*, "Energy is that which moves or quickens inert matter; a force or action communicated by vibrations or waves having its source in the human mind. Energy is an innate law from the beginning of creation that makes all particles comprehend, vibrate, oscillate, or shake at different speeds, subject to mind thought."

We are going to imbue the energy within a candle with our psychic energy and, when we light that candle, release kinetic energy to do our will.

The candle is our *potential* energy source. Each candle is

unique, the variations in color, shape, wax composition, and wick material all combine to form a unique product.

Our spirit is our psychic source. Psychic energy, again according to Dr. Bletzer, "...is an intelligent, powerful, invisible force formed by the friction of the blood cells running back and forth throughout the veins and arteries filling the body with electricity that is capable of being controlled and directed by the human mind."

When we combine the energy potential of the candle with the psychic energy of our spirit, we create a force that will influence the universe around us, subject to our will.

This brings us to the subject of the ethics involved in magick.

Ethics

When you use Candle Magick, you initiate changes in the universe.

There are constructive and destructive changes that you can make. Notice we did not say "good" or "bad" changes or positive or negative changes.

The universal energies are neutral, and therefore neither white (good forces) or black (evil forces), as depicted in fiction novels.

As an example, to stop a debilitating illness, one must use the destructive forces. This would be viewed as a *good* or healing act. However, these same forces, channeled to destroy or infect a healthy creature would be viewed as being wrong or a *bad* act.

Both of these acts set up karma for the initiator. Both use the very same energy from the universe. The only difference is how the power is used and the repercussions to the originator.

The deliberate and often ignorant abuse of power and magick is not isolated to race, color, creed, sexual preference, or religious belief. This is why metaphysical training and the laws of the universe are so important.

As a practitioner of magick, you have a great responsibility to yourself and to others to use your knowledge in a constructive and healing way.

Since the use or misuse of this energy is your prerogative, let us help you if we can toward making the proper and informed choice.

While we do not believe in the harming of others, we definitely do not believe in being anyone's victim or martyr. Furthermore, we would not expect anyone else to be either.

Doing unto others is a moral issue with which each of you must come to terms for yourself. What is right for us or others may not necessarily be right for you.

Which brings us to a very important point. It is our firm belief, as practitioners and teachers of metaphysics, that a student cannot grow magickally by being sheltered. One must be given the opportunity to grow into a karmically responsible practitioner of magick.

This means having the knowledge of both the constructive and destructive sides of magick, along with the ability to make a competent choice between the two. We, therefore, introduce you not only to the basics of constructive magick but to destructive magick as well. We do this mainly to insure the avoidance of innocent error and to provide for self defense, but also to provide for your spiritual growth by introducing you to different paths from which to choose.

As a practitioner of magick, be aware that the further you progress, the more rapidly you will receive the karma for your actions. It cannot be overemphasized that hexing, cursing, and jinxing are neither mere superstitions nor entertainments. Once done, they are difficult to undo. The backlash, if your victim is innocent of wrongdoing, is severe. Even if your victim is not innocent but has a strong auric shield and other means of protection, such as the Mirror of Reflection, that same hex, curse, or jinx could wind up back on you, possibly threefold.

Think very carefully before using this type of magick. If these methods must be used, and we admit that there are such times, be sure you first have exhausted all other avenues of action. Primarily make certain that you are innocent of any wrongdoing by being completely honest with yourself about the situation. Usually you will find that the fault is mutual.

REMEMBER

The Wiccan Rede: "And it harm none, do as you will."

Karmic Law

In her *Psychic Dictionary*, Dr. June Bletzer provides the best overall descriptions of the karmic spectrum that we have come across. They are reprinted here with her permission.

Karma (Sanskrit, Buddhism, Theosophy)—the principle that makes every man or woman the cause of their present global location, lifestyle, intelligence, relatives, and physical body condition; this principle is governed by one's entire activities, thoughts, and emotions throughout all incarnations; 1. A law of action: (a) for every action there is a reaction; (b) action and its fruits; (c) deeds, acts, and attitudes of one resulting in future deeds, acts, and attitudes, making one completely responsible for oneself; 2. Karma represents the sum total of the causes one has set into motion in past lives, making the pattern for this life and for future lives; this pattern can be changed, and rearranged purposely through preplanned deeds, acts, and attitudinal changes; 3. Karma works in one's favor or against one, doling out good or poor physical bodies and experiences; while living the results of the past, one is processing the condition of the future.

Karmic Debt (Sanskrit)—an unpleasant and uncomfortable experience one must go through to learn a lesson one did not learn, to compensate for something one should not have done, or to compensate for something one left undone, in one of their past incarnations or in the past of their present life.

Karmic Propensities—lower desires and thoughts which come from the *subconscious mind*, instigated from past lives; the logical mind will not consciously allow the person to carry them out, thus causing an uneasiness not thoroughly understood.

In summation, there is always a positive and better way of doing something than bringing harm or hardship to another. Karmic lessons are not a punishment, but given to us to enhance our learning and spiritual growth process. By these lessons, we learn that we are all a part of a giant whole. When we hurt another, we have also hurt ourselves.

Domino Effect

All magick is a combination of events designed to effect change. From the beginning of the magickal act to the final resultant action, great care must be taken to ensure that each step is guided with the ultimate goal in mind. Hasty preparation, lack of concentration, improper timing, and incorrect color usage can divert your magick from its intended path.

As in the domino theory, where action by one domino results in an action to and a reaction from the next domino in line, so too your magick, as it proceeds, affects each and every aspect of the universe it encounters. Proper preparation is the key to working magick correctly.

TEST YOUR KNOWLEDGE

THE LAWS OF CAUSE AND EFFECT

TRUE OR FALSE

1. We live in a sea of energy.
2. It is possible to alter the energy within an object with our minds.
3. If we combine the energy potential of the candle with the psychic energy of our mind, we create a force that will have little or no influence on the world around us.
4. Since everything is composed of varying degrees of living energy, the mind can influence these energies to mold and reshape reality.
5. Destructive energy is evil and should never be used under any circumstances.
6. The Law of Karma applies only to those who

understand and believe in it.

7. The teaching of magick should be limited to constructive magick only so as to protect others from themselves and karma.

8. The Domino Theory, as used in *The Candle Magick Workbook*, illustrates how to align your magickal work in order to hit a specific goal or target.

9. Candle Magick is a means of concentrating and focusing your will in a logical, step-by-step sequence, to achieve your magickal goals.

FOR YOUR NOTES

TEST YOUR KNOWLEDGE

ANSWER SHEET

1. True
2. True
3. False—We create an object of great influence on the world around us.
4. True
5. False—"To help stop a debilitating illness you must use the destructive forces."
6. False—Everything is subject to the Law of Karma.
7. False—You could not protect yourself nor could you heal disease without destructive magick.
8. True
9. True

2

Defining Your Magickal Goals and Results

If you could manifest anything into your life, what would it be? A new job, new home, more money? Can you envision yourself as having the items of your desire? Stop a moment and see if you can get a mental picture of what it is you want. How much detail can you see in this mental picture?

Write down, in as much detail as you can, each of the items you would like. Put only one item on a worksheet and place it in a binder. By writing your goals and desires on the worksheet and placing it in a binder, you have taken the first step toward obtaining them. This can be thought of as the *formation* stage, as you are now truly looking at what it is you want.

The real trick, however, is to determine how you want to realize your desires, and from what source. This is very important, and cannot be left to the fates or to the universe. As an example, you need money, and create a chant to that effect.

Money, money,
come to me,
and send me on
a spending spree

Now, this is good for knowing what you want, but you have left yourself wide open as to how it will come. All too often the desired "money" comes from sources that you would never have imagined: auto accidents, falls, lawsuits, insurance claims, the lottery, etc. Spend a few extra minutes to get clear on where or how you want this goal or desire to manifest itself. It pays off in the long run.

The *incubation* stage of this process begins as you prepare your magickal work. You have your goal and the results you desire in mind as you prepare to release this energy into the universe for manifestation. This is a time of drawing great power and energy to you, due to your concentration and the very act of preparing your magickal work. This work will ultimately be released to the universe in what is called a thought form as you light your candle.

From your binder, remove the most important item you want to manifest and the corresponding result and source of this manifestation. Study these carefully, as you will need this information later.

A special note here: you will find, as many people do, that writing down what it is you want in life can be difficult. We often want it all right now. The worksheet will help you to focus your energies, one at a time, on only the most important of these goals, better defining any problems that may be preventing you from having what you want. It will aid your concentration and help you isolate a source to manifest your desires or goals.

TEST YOUR KNOWLEDGE

MAGICKAL GOALS

EXERCISES

1. Write on the sheet of paper called "For Your Notes" at the end of this section something you want to manifest.
2. Now, write HOW you would like to receive this manifestation.
3. Next, state clearly from WHERE exactly this manifestation is to come from.
4. Reduce the manifestation instructions to a short rhyme that includes HOW you are to receive it and from WHERE it is to come.
5. Repeat #1 through #4 above with a second manifestation desire.

FOR YOUR NOTES

TEST YOUR KNOWLEDGE

ANSWER SHEET

1. Exercise—Write in as much detail as possible. Take your time. This is a fun exercise so enjoy yourself. Remember, as you think, you create.
2. Exercise—What form will it take?
3. Exercise—From what source?
4. Exercise—Try to limit this to six to nine lines at first. Then weed out the extra words.
5. Self-explanatory.

PART THREE

Imagination is the highest kite one can fly.

—Lauren Bacall, born 1924

1

Communicating With the Candle

The candle itself can be equated to the human body or human potential. It is composed of the magickal elements of Earth, Air, and Water. Once energized and lit, Fire and Spirit are added: All the elements necessary for magick and life embodied in, one compact unit. Refer to candle illustration on next page.

The Symbology of the Candle

Will

The energy you place into the candle is the unseen factor that creates change in accordance with your desires. That which gives shape and life to an action leading to an ultimate reaction. Will is symbolized by a properly energized and lit candle. Elemental Kingdom—a thought form created by the magickian.

27

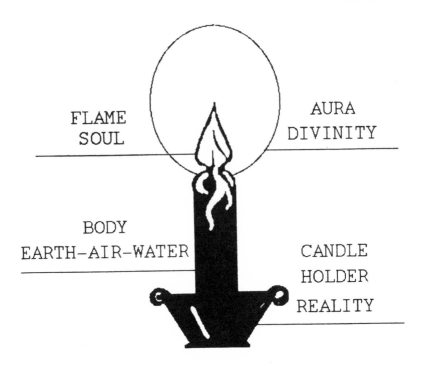

Halo

The aura or halo around the flame represents divinity achieved, the life hereafter, the transmuted state to the God-self. Elemental Kingdom—all on a spiritual level only.

The Body

The physical properties of the candle exclusive of the wicking. Whether you use a vegetable wax, a tallow or petroleum base, oil or bees wax, all the elements are brought to bear when the candle is lit. When unlit, all elements are present except Fire, Spirit and Will (if undedicated). Elemental Kingdoms—as indicated above.

Flame

The flame of the candle represents the seat of the soul. The spirit's transcendence and knowledge of its own divinity. Elemental Kingdom—salamanders. (Each tiny flame houses a living salamander.)

Wicking

The wicking represents the human potential when unlit. Once lit, it becomes the vehicle by which transmutation is made possible. Symbolized by the rising of the Kundalini. Elemental Kingdom—gnomes when unlit, sylphs and salamanders when lit.

Candle Holder

The candle holder represents reality as we perceive it along with all that contains and sustains us here on Mother Earth. Elemental Kingdom—Earth/gnomes.

The Altar

The Altar and Circle (Optional)

The altar, within the magickal circle, represents the Sun or being one with the divine self. It is the representation of divine magick and a recognition of one's own immortality and divinity.

Since most altar setups require at least a representation of the four elements of Earth, Air, Fire, and Water, the single candle can be seen as embodying all of these. Thus, further regalia is not necessary, but is a luxury.

Setting Up an Altar

Altar setups are limited only by your imagination. You simply need a quiet, safe place to work. Begin with a sturdy table, chest, or dresser that is of sufficient height to prevent children and pets from tipping over any items you place upon it, and of sufficient weight to prevent it from being easily tipped over.

Once you have the table in place, consider what items you will require to perform your magick. Will you be needing a basic or elaborate setting? Perhaps you want it to be inconspicuous?

To help you in your selection and setup, we have briefly described three generic altars. They will give you a basic working knowledge of how to construct and tailor the altar to your specific needs.

Simple Altar

Upon whatever you have selected for your base, place a thick piece of glass. The glass protects your altar from wax and other items that might damage the base.

Place upon the altar a candle representing your purpose. This is commonly called a Petition or Purpose Candle. It represents what you are manifesting.

Protect this candle by placing it within a decorative but fireproof container that you have partially filled with a base of sea sand and baking soda or whatever you feel will support the candle but will not catch fire.

Use a small wooden or clay box to store your lighter, incense, and oils. Your incense stick can be placed in the candle container, embedded into the sand beside your candle. Thus the fireproof container doubles as an incense burner as well. You now have created a simple but serviceable altar that is every bit as good as the most elaborate.

One more point to consider when constructing any altar is its alignment with the compass. All Candle Magick is done when facing the direction which will govern the magick at hand. For this reason, many altars are circular and placed in the middle of the room. Simply align your altar so that you are aware of the correct directions for North, South, East, and West.

The Elaborate Altar

Any simple altar can be made more elaborate by placing items upon it that define the quarters. The quarters are simply the four directions of North, East, South, and West.

To define the North, you might place a pentacle or scourge on the altar. For the East, a censor or wand. For the South, a sword or athame. For the West, a small cauldron or cup.

Remember, anything that relates to one of the four directions or quarters can be used on your altar to represent that specific energy. Be inventive. A potted plant can be used for the North, an owl feather for the East, a lava rock for the South, and a goldfish in a bowl for the West. We use figurines of a wolf for the North, an owl for the East, a lioness for the South, and a dolphin for the West. Use what has a special meaning for you.

THE LANGUAGE OF CANDLES

As you begin working with candles, you will discover that they have a unique language. The language is expressed by the dancing of the flame, the wafting of the smoke, and the snap and crackle of the burning wax. In order to successfully interpret how your magickal work is progressing, you will need to become familiar with candle language. You will be communicating not only with your own subconscious, but with the Fire Elementals as well.

No two candles will ever react the same way when lit even when they are homemade and all things are known to be equal in their manufacture. Though undedicated, a candle has unique properties that individualize it from others of the same batch. When dedicated and lit, each candle displays its unique personality (shaped from your desires) that is communicated by the tiny Fire Element or salamander housed within the flame. Communication with you will vary slightly from candle to candle depending on the task assigned it and how well you have aligned your dominoes.

As your candle burns, free your mind and concentrate on the candle. Watch how the smoke rises and the flame dances and listen to the sounds it makes. The smoke may rise to the East or waft to the South, the flame may flare or dwindle, and the sounds may be of a popping nature. Ask yourself how these actions relate to the magick you are performing. The answers you perceive are often startling and revealing about the true nature of your desires.

Do not be surprised if the unenlightened attribute the language of your candles to the myriad of "logical" explanations regarding drafts, chemical compositions, atmospheric conditions, etc. When the results are in and heads are scratched in dismay, just remember that "All of Magick Is a Seeming Array of Uncanny Coincidence to the Unenlightened."

The Flame

You will soon realize that your candle flame will frequently wave, dip, and bob regardless of how carefully you shield it against drafts. This is called a dancing flame, one of the ways a candle communicates with you. The dance has meaning and, once understood, can help you determine how your magick is progressing.

A Strong Flame: This indicates that power and energy are going into your desires for manifestation. This is a very good sign. When a figure candle is used, a strong flame generally indicates that the person represented by the figure is winning or angry or is using authority over another. When two figure candles are present, the higher and stronger flame represents authority over the other.

A Weak Flame: This can show that you are facing heavy opposition and must redo the magick several times in order to overcome the power you are facing. The weak flame can also indicate, on a figure candle, that the subject is losing the battle, argument, etc., against another.

The weak flame that goes out usually means that you have missed your target altogether. Start over and be more careful of the domino alignment and energy imbuing.

A Jumping Flame: This is an attention getter. It can indicate raw emotions along with explosions of energy, depending on the candle used and its intended purpose.

When two figure candles are being used, a jumping flame usually means that an energetic or heated discussion or argument is taking place.

The Rainbow Flame: As indicated by the name, this flame is composed of various colors. They have the same meanings as those listed in the COLOR section in this workbook (pages 89–97).

We feel here that an example is in order, since when you are being taught something, you assimilate the information better if you are shown an example.

Turn to page 143 and review the part under LOVE. You are manifesting love and have lit your candle. The flame is tall and flickers at its tip, and leans heavily first to the West and then to the North.

In our example, the flicker can indicate excitement and communication to come since this is Candle Magick done on a waxing Moon.

The flame that leans to the West indicates the strong emotions involved, and that this is indeed love magick. There may even be a small amount of Pink, Blue, or Silver in the flame.

The flame then leans heavily to the North indicating a manifestation of your desires.

The following general rules apply to the above example with regard to the direction of flame movement:

North
   On a waxing Moon, something physical is manifesting. In this case, it is love.

East
   Something mental is manifesting. Had the flame leaned to the East in the above example, it could have meant that you had someone in mind you wanted as a partner in love. The flickering could mean a forthcoming conversation.

South

Had the flame leaned toward the South, you could expect a steamy love affair, perhaps though of short duration, depending upon other signs. The flame leaning to the South and then to the North would have indicated a love of long duration, more stable, possibly even a marriage.

West

As the flame in our example leaned toward the West first, it was an acknowledgment of the emotional aspect of the magick. A very good sign of success, particularly in love magick.

To illustrate one of several other methods in employing the language of the candle, review page 153 of your workbook entitled "Send Away Tired Feelings."

Presume that this is the magick you are performing. Let's look at what action the smoke might take and what meaning it could have for you.

The smoke rises rapidly from an orange-tipped flame that is still, tall, and very strong. The smoke wafts first toward you and covers you with a gray-white cloud, then flutters away to the South.

In this example, the smoke acknowledged your request by covering you with the cloud. It then displayed the direction it was taking the petition to; in this case, the South in order to manifest more energy for you.

The following general rules apply when interpreting the direction your candle smoke takes:

North

You will have to work for what you want. Success will not be easy or rapid. Perseverance is the key here. In the case of health, it can mean a condition can get worse. Look to other omens for more information.

East

Success comes with thought and strategy. Carefully review the situation. Patience is the key here.

South

Success comes rapidly with your request. In the case of health, your recovery is immanent.

West

When the smoke wafts to the West, the issue is too emotional. Step back. You are too involved. Look at the situation from a detached point of view to clear the mind. Then, reanalyze the problem. Is there something you are overlooking?

THE TALKING CANDLE

Candle chatter denotes communication on some level. That level will depend upon the magick you are performing. Chatter is most common when using figure candles and can denote who is getting told what and by whom.

Soft, Infrequent Chatter: Indicates intimate conversation and, at times, pure thoughts.

Mild, Frequent Chatter: Someone in a position of authority is giving orders or directions.

Strong, Frequent Chatter: Denotes arguments, quarrels, or loud disagreements.

Remember, the language of the candle is important. The direction of the flame, the wafting of the smoke, and the audible chatter all are a form of communication for divination into past, current, and future events. Take notes and learn the language of the candle so you can better understand the workings of your magick.

Whenever you are looking for omens in the candle language, always use your common sense. Remember that each magickal act is different and each candle is unique. Combine this awareness with your subconscious interpretations of the omens and you will find that your interpretations will vary from those of others under similar circumstances. Experiment to find what is right for you.

FOR YOUR INFORMATION

Blowing Out Candles: If the flame is to be extinguished before the candle burns away completely, the candle should always be smothered. Blowing out the flame is an affront to the Fire Elements.

Double Wick Candles: You will find that some candles come

with a double wick. This is intentional and not a manufacturing error. These double wicks are used with Confusion Oil against enemies or to confuse an issue. A double wick is also used to confuse and stall a situation until you can make other plans or arrangements.

Matches: These should never be used to light a magickal candle. Try to use a perpetual flame, another candle, incense, or a lighter. The sulfur and phosphorus have traditionally been used in destructive magick. Brimstone is another term for this.

Old Broken Candles: In a magickal situation, never use a candle that has been broken or burnt. A broken candle will not conduct energy properly and one used previously in any fashion has already been programmed by another's energy.

Relighting a Candle: Never relight a candle that goes out by itself. By going out, the candle is telling you that either your magick is concluded or you have done it improperly.

Safety First: As with any potentially dangerous element, some common sense precautions could save your life.

1. Always keep a small fire extinguisher within arms reach of your altar or candle setup.
2. Always keep your candle within a container of sea sand and baking soda or use, as we do, a layer of Johnny Cat, even if it is housed in a heat resistant glass. The glass gets very hot as the candle burns.
3. There should be a five to six-inch clearance from the flame tip to the top of your container.
4. Always keep a metal screen covering the candle container to prevent whiskers and tiny fingers from painful burns.
5. Be sure to place your candle on a sturdy table or altar, in a fireplace, or anywhere it will not cause a fire if it falls over.
6. Try to work skyclad (nude) when working with the fire elementals. Robes and such should be flame retardant if used.

TEST YOUR KNOWLEDGE

COMMUNICATING WITH THE CANDLE

TRUE OR FALSE

1. The candle can be equated to the human body or human potential.
2. The chattering flame often represents a candle's speech.
3. A dancing flame just indicates that a draft is present.
4. Smoke wafting about your candle indicates mental action.
5. The energized candle does not have a life of its own, therefore it cannot communicate and its odd mannerisms are of no consequence.

FOR YOUR NOTES

TEST YOUR KNOWLEDGE

ANSWER SHEET

1. True
2. True
3. False—A dancing flame is a significant indication of how well your magick is progressing and what it may be up against.
4. True
5. False—The combination of the elementals embodied within your candle, your subconscious, and your will, create a limited life form. This basic unit of life can be communicated with and is part of the elemental kingdom. It is not a true thought form, however.

2

Dressing Your Candle

Candle Without Glass Enclosures

While facing in the direction that best corresponds to your magickal needs, place a small portion of your chosen oil or perfume onto your palms. Rub your palms together briskly until you feel them slide freely and warm slightly.

Mentally see your candle as divided into two sections, upper (wick end) and lower (holder end). Visualize where the middle dividing line might be, an imaginary midpoint.

Grasp your candle with your right hand, just above the midpoint, and with your left hand, just below the midpoint. Once your hands are properly placed, be sure that your palms are in contact with the candle at all times.

Stand with your feet flat on the floor. Hold your candle approximately chest high and concentrate on your purpose and your desire.

Envision Gold light from Mother Earth entering into your feet from below and circulating up through your body.

Next, visualize Pearlesque energy from the Universe entering at the top of your head.

Now, envision both of these energies swirling around you in increasing speed, building up power and energy within your body and aura until they seem difficult to contain.

Feel all this energy concentrating within your hands. Feel your hands grow hot with energy and power. Feel them begin to pulsate, almost throbbing.

Begin stroking the candle by moving the right hand upward from the midpoint. While doing so, continue to concentrate on your purpose and desire. At the same time, envision the light energy pouring into the candle from your palms. When your right hand reaches the top of the candle, release the candle and regrasp it at the midpoint.

When the right hand regrasps the midpoint, begin a downward stroke with the left hand to the base, then release the candle and regrasp it at the midpoint.

Continue stroking with alternate hands until you sense this energy exploding outward from the depths of the candle. The candle at this point is fully energized.

When your candle is properly energized, you will have an inner sense of peace and calm. Almost a state of euphoria. You will personally feel empowered and invigorated. There will be no doubt that your candle has been properly prepared.

With regular use, you will soon find the visualizations and energies becoming a physical as well as a mental sensation. Intense concentration and a strong will to succeed are necessary to properly imbue your candle with light energy of sufficient intensity to accomplish your purpose and desire. If you cannot feel, sense, or visualize your candle as described, you have not sufficient power or will to manifest what you want.

If doubt still lingers, redo the candle energizing technique and proceed with your Magickal Act. Do not let insecurity get you down. Magick requires the proper channeling of energy, not confidence. Confidence often comes only with experience. Do not worry if your magick is going to work or not. That worry in itself can prevent your candle from doing its work properly.

Anointing the Glass Encased Candle

To properly energize a candle encased by glass or some other material, follow all the steps as outlined in the procedure for non-encased candles but with a few minor alterations to accommodate the container.

Instead of palming your oils and rubbing them into the candle body, thus energizing the oil and the candle at the same time, energize your oil separately. Then pour the oils into the container atop the candle. Proceed with your visualization as before.

The Key to Successful Magick

If we seem redundant and you read this admonition elsewhere in the workbook, it is only that we feel it is so important that you realize that the key to successful Candle Magick rests on your ability to concentrate your will while visualizing the goal. Above all, release your emotions. Energizing your candle is the appropriate time to release all anger, love, pain, or desire. Release the appropriate emotion to enhance your act. These released emotions are the artists for your magickal act, while the light energies are the medium with which these artists will work. When the candle is lit, it releases a work of art into the Universe for manifestation. (See Advanced Techniques of Candle Energizing in Part Nine.)

3

The Pendulum as a Gauge

To test the power and energy within any candle, try using a pendulum. This is one of the special tools we use to check on how well we have imbued a candle, and as a gauge for determining Chakra health, pinpointing illness within the body, advice gathering, and a multitude of others.

Dangle the pendulum above the candle and pose the question, "How much energy is within this candle?" Try this first on a non-energized candle. What kind of response did you get? The pendulum should move in answer. The direction of movement is not important at this time, but the amount of movement should be noted and used as a reference point.

Now energize your candle but do not light it yet. Again pose your question while dangling the pendulum over the candle. Notice a difference? Large? Small? If the difference is significant, you have done a good job of energizing your candle.

Now light your candle, complete your magickal act, and then pose the same question. This time the movement of the pendulum should be much stronger then either of the two previous times you gauged it.

With a little imagination, the pendulum can be used to measure energy in all your magickal acts. You then never will have to worry about putting enough energy into a candle because you will be gauging your own progress.

As we previously stated, the direction of the pendulum's swing is not as important as the range. You may, however, want to know a little more about the type of energy present.

Generally, a clockwise motion indicates constructive energy; a counterclockwise motion, destructive energy. A forward and back motion usually means "yes" while a left to right motion represents "no." Yours will possibly vary as the pendulum is a method of communicating with your inner Child and Higher Self.

Do not be discouraged if the pendulum does not respond immediately to your questions. As in all magick, expertise in using any tool comes with repeated practice.

TEST YOUR KNOWLEDGE

DRESSING YOUR CANDLE

TRUE OR FALSE

1. You need not face any specific direction when dressing and energizing your candle.
2. When dressing your candle, the right hand strokes the candle from the midpoint upward.
3. When dressing a glass encased candle, such as a Novena, place a generous amount of oil onto the palms of your hands and anoint the exterior case of the candle.
4. To properly energize a candle, as taught in this workbook, you must become a channel for energy.
5. The success or failure of Candle Magick lies in your ability to focus your will into the candle.

FOR YOUR NOTES

TEST YOUR KNOWLEDGE

ANSWER SHEET

1. False—Always face the direction that most pertains to the elements and magick being used.
2. True
3. False
4. True
5. True

PART FOUR

"... the most profound relationship we'll ever have is the one with ourselves."

—Shirley MacLaine, born 1934

1

Developing Your Magickal Power

THE PROCESS

We cannot emphasize enough the importance of the Aura and Chakras in magick. These two single items, beyond vegetarianism and a physical discipline such as Yoga, Akido, or Ti Chi, are of primary importance to the serious practitioner of magick. The Aura is your shield and protection, while the Chakras are energy centers that are vital for manifesting your will in magick. You need to be both clean and in balance for serious magickal and spiritual work. These areas are cleansed through a process called Creative Visualization. But, before you can clean the Aura and work with the Chakras, you must get the cooperation of your three inner selves and get to know something about Creative Visualization.

Our Three Selves

Hidden within each of us are three distinct natures called the Child Self, the Middle Self, and the Higher Self. These three natures must be in balance and harmony for one to live a rich and fulfilling life. When these are functioning properly, life seems easier and you feel lucky, since everything good seems to come your way.

If one of these inner selves is out of balance, then all are misaligned. Your life will seem difficult and unlucky. You will feel helpless to prevent misfortune. You may also feel cut off from others, suspicious, and irritable. Everyone seems to be taking advantage of you.

The Child Self

As children, we often lived moment by moment in different worlds of fantasy and make believe. We could entertain ourselves for hours, lost in wondrous places that we created from within our being. We felt excited by life and its many wonders. Then, self-renewal was continuous.

But at some point in life, we become so grown up that we forget how to dream and fantasize; how to enjoy just being alive. Was it when our parents first chided us for our overactive imaginations? Or when we became so bogged down in our everyday lives that we were too tired to care? For some of us, there never was a childhood. We seem to have been born adults with adult shortsightedness.

Whenever it was that you lost contact with that inner child, it is vital that you reconnect and heal him or her. If your life is an emotional mess and relationships are poor, look to your inner Child Self.

To illustrate, consider children of two or three years of age. Would you abuse them by cursing and swearing at them? Would you punish them for trying yet failing at a task?

Well, that is exactly what we do all the time to our inner Child Self. We curse ourselves, call ourselves names, and become thoroughly disgusted when we fail. Let's face it. Much of the time we hate or abuse ourselves. We complain about not being handsome, beautiful, rich, charming, witty, or intelligent. So what prevents us from achieving those traits? Aside from having the physical traits judged to be handsome or beautiful, it is we ourselves who tell us we are not handsome, beautiful or witty. And we hate ourselves for it.

How do we remedy this? By working with this small child called the unconscious or subconscious mind. Freud referred to it as the Id. The Kahunas call it the Animal Self. By whatever name, this tiny being that shares our body cannot speak, so it communicates only by pictures and emotions. So when we strongly curse ourselves, it obligingly helps us do just that. Being of simple mind and wanting to please, it calls to the Higher Self for the energy to manifest our wish. This is why one continually hears that we manifest our own reality. We are cocreators of our universe.

Our every thought, as you will see, appears in a variety of places, such as the Aura. Our Child Self, dealing in symbolism, promptly places our desires and emotions as symbols into our Aura through our Chakras. It's like being a neon sign saying "Kick me, I deserve it" or "I deserve money, love and happiness." These symbols attract or repel just that energy from our Higher Self, others around us and the universe. That is why you must watch your words, emotions, and thoughts. You would be quite surprised at the garbage you can accumulate.

When you say or think something destructive, or someone else says anything hurtful to you, say to yourself, "Cancel," "Erase," or something similar. This will have a surprising effect. It could be your code word to your Child Self to ignore that last statement. This shields your inner child from thoughtless words or acts. By stating to yourself that you will not accept that which you do not deserve, you maintain your individuality and are guilt free.

Guilt is one of those items that friends and family love to hang on our Auras like a tree decoration. Guilt is a tool for manipulating and stealing one's power and energy. By rejecting such actions, the Aura stays cleaner. You will not manifest in your life lessons you do not deserve nor will you be at the mercy of others.

Now that you know what to do or not to do, how do you

communicate with your Child Self? Gently and with great patience. Patience is the key to guiding and teaching your inner child how to please you. It truly does not know why, nor does it understand, that when it does exactly as requested it sometimes displeases you.

To demonstrate this, look inside yourself. Call to your Child Self and be patient. Remember, you have given this little child years of abuse along with what it has received from the outside world. Every time someone has hurt you or has made you cry, they have hurt your inner child. Expect that child to be shy at first.

As your inner child appears to you, it may appear frightened or battered. Be loving and understanding. Remember it has the mentality of a two- or three-year-old and no more. If the inner child does not come right away, keep trying. Do not worry.

More than likely, it will appear when you are in a relaxed state and your mind is not so congested with other thoughts. Be patient. It will appear when the time is right. Watch your dreams. Frequently, this is where the child will come to you first; then, later, when you are creatively visualizing.

When the child appears, tell it you are sorry for any abuse. Ask it to teach you how to love and communicate with it. As with any child, the outpouring of love and emotions will be so great you may have trouble containing it. So don't! Don't contain the emotions! Let the child express them! Remember, that is why you called the child in the first place. The typical reaction of tears and a big hug is nothing to be ashamed of. Who are there but you and the child anyway?

You will likely feel a sudden release of emotions along with a myriad of pictures of old hurts. Walk the child through these hurts as you would a son or daughter. Talk to the child as you would a loved one, realizing it doesn't understand hurt and pain. Help it to overcome these destructive emotions. It will respond. By doing this, you will find that your temper cools quickly and people will be unable to hurt you as easily or deeply. Your life suddenly becomes smoother and calmer. When you have questions in life, answers seem to come from nowhere. You find your ESP increasing. There is an inner attitude change taking place. Knowledge you did not know you possessed surfaces. And, best of all, you have just gained years on most practitioners of magick.

This is a truth that few realize. Your Child Self is the key to extrasensory perception, to obtaining the proper energies you require to manifest magick into your life. Your Child Self feels your emotions, recognizes your magickal symbols, then seeks the Higher Self for the energies you have asked for. Remember, words do not mean anything. It is the emotion that follows symbols that the inner child understands. That is why you must be specific and sincere when you deal with this child.

With this child's cooperation, you can practice divination, psychometry, and dowsing, cast runes, read tarot, perform Candle Magick, interpret dreams, and much more. The reason for this is that metaphysics uses symbolism for communication.

The Higher Self

Your Higher Self regulates your spirituality and growth. It is in regular communication with your Child Self. This higher being allows you to cross the threshold of being a mere mortal, to experience divine consciousness. It is responsible for miracles, wisdom, and the knowledge of right from wrong. It sends the energy to you requested through your Child Self.

The higher nature does not condemn nor condone. It simply observes and will make suggestions. A frequent statement by the higher nature when you have a problem is . . . "Well, have you thought of . . ." and it goes on to give you a different perspective of the situation. At no time does it tell you what to do. It will always ask you questions until you derive the answer or acquire another perspective.

The Higher Self can be male or female at your request. It is the sum total of who and what you are from all lifetimes. It is not bound by our three-dimensional plane and will be your biggest ally for exploring past lives and obtaining lost wisdom.

The Middle Self

The Middle Self is discussed after the Higher Self as it is your personality, your ego in this life. It is your conscious being, the face you see in the mirror, the essence of who you are now.

It is the function of the Middle Self to coordinate the energies between your Higher and Lower Selves. In other words, the ego must learn to communicate with the Child or Lower Self for its needs. The Child Self then encodes this into the Aura via the Chakras and sends the message to the Higher Self. In return, the Higher Self sends the energies to the Child Self via the same route for manifestation. This is a cooperative effort where each one helps the other.

So closely linked is this process that the Hawaiian Kahuna Magickal systems teach that each body has three distinct selves. Each of these selves or spirits is separate and is linked for a single lifetime into one body. It is the job of each spirit to teach and help the others progress until each has gone from a Child Self, mute within the body, to a Middle Self, with all the complex decisions of life, to the Higher Self, that must not judge but maintain an impartial and unbiased nature.

Finally, to further demonstrate the interrelationships here, let us create the perfect person. If all three aspects of Self are functioning at optimum with excellent communications, we would have a Christ, Buddha, or Demigod.

EXAMPLES OF PERSONALITY TYPES

The Criminal

When the Higher Self is cut off from the Middle Self and the Child Self, there is no sense of right or wrong. Further, there is no sense of relationship or connection (feeling) for others. This person would probably be the hardened criminal type that has cut off the channel leading from the top of the head (the Crown Chakra) to the Higher Self.

The Vegetable

When the ego or Middle Self withdraws from the trinity, we have a vegetable. There is nothing to connect the Higher Self and the Child Self. This person functions best as a child. On the other hand, he or she may think of himself or herself as a saint or higher alter ego in an attempt to fill the void left by the ego. Trauma can cause the ego to abandon the trinity.

The Self Destructive

When the Child Self can no longer take abuse or strain, it shuts down the various systems of the body. This, of course, eventually leads to death. Since the Child Self regulates all autonomic functions of the body, it is capable of healing or destroying as it sees fit.

SUMMARY

What we have attempted to demonstrate here by dealing with each of the inner selves is the necessity of working with all of yourself to your fullest capacity. In doing so, you will be putting yourself years ahead on the path of spirituality and magick. This knowledge will expand into your everyday life, making it richer, fuller, and much happier.

Finally, it is important for you to realize that magick can be done without recognizing the relative relationships of the three selves, but you may be severely handicapped in your efforts.

As an example, understanding how the child nature functions and what its purpose is will help ensure your magickal success. To ignore this inner nature and how it communicates will result only in a hit or miss technique. Without you knowing this inner nature's speech is emotion and its alphabet is symbol, your magick will be mediocre at best.

Learning the interaction of the three selves within you and how they interconnect to the Aura, Chakras, and the physical body is understanding how true magick works. This knowledge will become invaluable in understanding later relationships in Candle Magick, your spiritual progression, and Creative Visualization.

TEST YOUR KNOWLEDGE

DEVELOPING YOUR MAGICKAL POWER

MIXED QUIZ

1. Name the three selves described in the workbook.
2. The language of the Child Self is symbol. (True or False)
3. The Higher Self is always male. (True or False)
4. The Ego or Middle Self maintains all unconscious body functions. (True or False)
5. Doing successful Candle Magick does not entirely depend on learning about the inner selves, but it helps. (True or False)

FOR YOUR NOTES

2

Creative Visualization

Creative Visualization is one of the magickian's most useful tools. This is the process of stilling the mind and allowing your three inner selves to align and work with you for desired information and manifestation. This information can come to you in a variety of forms—i.e., taste, smell, sound, feelings—but most often as mental symbols or pictures.

At first, the process of stilling the mind is difficult as the child within you suddenly gets a chance to air his or her dissatisfactions. So expect a thousand different distractions. To still these distractions, call to the small child within you. Calm the child and take care of its needs whatever they might be. Once the Child Self is happy, it is ready to help you.

Make helping you a game. All children love games and your child nature is no different. Explain what it is you wish to do. Put as much thought (pictures) and emotion behind it as possible.

Explain that you wish to visualize, without interruption, the cleansing of the aura and chakras. Since this is an easy and

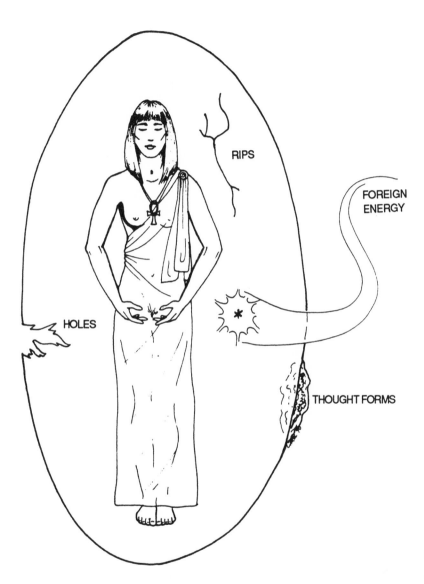

VISUALIZING YOUR AURIC SHIELD

pleasant task, your Child Self should have no problem with the following steps. If it does, this means there is unfinished business and you need to work further with your child nature. Be sure it is not too tired, hungry, or thirsty or you will not be able to work effectively. Listen to it if it warns that this is not a good time. Begin to trust in its foreknowledge if it tells you to turn off the phone or something of a like nature.

There is a fine line between Creative Visualization, Meditation, Self-Hypnosis, and Day Dreaming (Fantasies). Some claim the line is so fine it is not worth mentioning.

- *Creative Visualization*: A semi-controlled day dream or fantasy state that eventually leads the practitioner into an altered state of awareness. It is used extensively in magick and healing. It is often a light combination of all three methods described below, which gives this method its popularity.
  Key Words: semi-controlled state of awareness.
- *Meditations*: A deep controlled state of mental and physical altered awareness. Meditation is usually a spiritual and physical discipline or philosophy.
Key Words: Controlled state of awareness.
- *Self-Hypnosis*: A method very similar to meditation with the exception that it is not considered a spiritual or physical discipline by itself. Nor does it follow a single philosophy or procedure as most meditations require. It is done primarily for self improvement and programming.
  Key Words: Self programming.
- *Day Dreams*: Uncontrolled flight of the mind and thought processes used mainly for escapism and therapy.
  Key Words: Uninhibited thought.

Breathing

Let's start first by analyzing your breathing technique.

Begin to breathe naturally. Place your hands on your stomach and then on your ribs. How do you breathe? In shallow breaths? Do you breathe just with your chest? Does it rise and fall while your stomach stays still? Perhaps your stomach rises and falls while your chest is stationary?

How you breathe is very important and will effect both your magick and any altered state of awareness you hope to achieve.

Shallow Upper Chest Breaths

Shallow breathers in our society are common and found to be highly stressed individuals. Often they lack proper circulation and have many aches and pains. There are more shallow upper chest breathers than lower abdominal breathers as our social norms dictate we hold our stomachs in. This is an unnatural state and results in the forced upper breathing motion.

Lower Abdominal Breathers

Lower abdominal breathing, the use of only half the lung capacity, again robs the individual of needed oxygen. Those who are lower abdominal breathers would also suffer from similar maladies as previously mentioned. They are usually found outside the United States where holding in the stomach is not necessarily a social requirement.

The Proper Way to Breath

Place your hands around your waist. See if you can breathe without lifting the chest or the stomach. Does your waist expand while the upper chest and stomach stay relatively motionless? Do you feel the upper and lower lung areas filling? Perhaps you feel a little light-headed?

This light-headed feeling is because you are not used to getting so much oxygen. Do not overdo it. Breathe comfortably and slowly and begin to integrate this full lung breathing into your everyday life and magickal practices. You will find you have more energy and your stress will be greatly reduced.

You will also find it is easier to stay in mental and physical contact with the magickal realms. With this method of breathing, every waking minute is a new and magickal experience as information and energy begin to flow freely.

Experiment and see what each method of breathing can do for you. Each has a different effect on the mind and body.

Each also affects how deeply you can achieve an altered state of awareness, which in turn affects your magickal progression.

TECHNIQUES WE USE

Now that you have a pretty good idea just what Creative Visualization is and how to breathe properly, let's try some of the techniques we use ourselves. As they become more familiar to you, we're sure you will vary them to suit your own personality and lifestyle.

First, select a quiet time and place, when and where you are least likely to be disturbed. If you have a separate room devoted to your magick, use this area. If necessary, place a "Do Not Disturb" sign on your door, turn off the phone, or turn on your answering machine. If you have small children that are not attending school yet, try to coincide your visualization time with their nap time. Also, be sure that all your electrical appliances have run their cycle or are turned off. There is nothing more distracting then a dishwasher or washing machine suddenly going to the rinse cycle and banging the wall or pipes. Oh yes, the coffee pot and curling irons should be checked. Firemen rushing through the house tends to disturb one's concentration.

Second, remove all tight clothing you are wearing. Leotards, jogging suits, sweats, or your birthday suit are ideal.

The next half hour or so will be devoted solely to you and your magickal growth. Try to make arrangements for at least this much time each day just for you. This may mean rising earlier or going to bed later. The time you spend will be well worth the effort as you will come to find an inner sense of peace and calm that you might never have known before. The stress that kept you awake at night and made you snappish melts away. You become a brighter and happier person. Problems seem much smaller and answers tend to come easier when you take just a few minutes to relax completely.

Now that you are alone in a quiet place where you will not be disturbed, sit or lie in a comfortable position. Be sure your neck and spine are properly supported to offer maximum comfort.

Take a comfortable but deep breath, filling both the upper

and lower parts of the lungs. Breathe in through your nose and hold this breath for as long as is comfortable for you.

Slowly release the breath to the mental count of ten while emitting a low hiss, sigh, or groan. Don't be shy about the noise. This is your release valve; use it! Repeat this deep breathing and vocal release several times. Give yourself permission to release any tension, anxiety, and all within you that does not serve your highest good. If you feel like crying, laughing, or chanting, do so. For a while, you will feel like a volcano finally erupting forth everything that has been held within. You will experience many emotions at this point and, as you proceed, allow them to come to the surface. Do not repress them. Look at them and let them go, knowing that these once were chains that bound you.

Repeat this process as often as you like. Each time, try to see with your mind just what is being exhaled from within your emotional being. Do faces of those who hurt or angered you appear? Is it the pain of injury or disease? As you grow you may be greatly surprised at what you can expel from your body and mind.

When this is properly done, a warm glow fills the body. You feel lighter, calmer, more serene. A feeling that you have accomplished something important fills you, as it should. It is not just anyone that is willing to release the past with all its hurts, sorrows, and bonds. Most people cling to these miseries like old and familiar shoes, unable to let go. But you are now different. You are learning how to let go.

Now continue breathing deeply and slowly. Ask yourself where a safe place would be for your inner magickal work. It can be any place you mentally create. Or a real place that you have been to before and can mentally recreate. Above all, it must be a place that you will feel safe and comfortable, where you can create magick and meet your teachers. Perhaps you envision a forest, a beach, a childhood treehouse or a fantasy land. Whatever you create, it is yours and yours alone.

Imagine now that there are ten steps either ascending or descending into your haven. Continuing to breath deeply and slowly, count each step as you approach the sanctuary. Explore your world. Who or what is there? A magickal teacher? Animals? Fairies? Whatever is there, this is your special place. For now, just observe, knowing that you can always come back for further exploration and needed rest anytime you wish. When you are ready to leave, just retrace your steps to where you began.

From this time forward, after you have released all emotions that no longer serve your highest good, go to your special place for healing and creative visualization work. It is a world between worlds and is every bit as real as the one in which you now physically exist. All meditations, visualizations, daydreams, and self-hypnosis problems can be safely taken there.

TEST YOUR KNOWLEDGE

CREATIVE VISUALIZATION

TRUE OR FALSE

1. Creative Visualization is one of the magickian's most useful tools.
2. Creative Visualization is an uncontrolled daydream.
3. Meditation is a mental and often times physical discipline.
4. Self-Hypnosis is very similar to meditation without the physical disciplines.
5. Learning proper breathing techniques is not important in Creative Visualization.

FOR YOUR NOTES

TEST YOUR KNOWLEDGE

ANSWER SHEET

1. True
2. False—Creative Visualization is a controlled day dream or fantasy leading to an altered state of awareness.
3. True
4. True
5. False—Learning proper breathing techniques is very important to inducting various levels of altered awareness.

3

The Aura

The Aura is the energy field that surrounds everything individually, both animate and inanimate. It is this field that records the history of an object or creature. Psychometrists can read this field of energy and those with auric vision can see it.

The auric field can be seen as a pulsating array of colors, shapes, and geometric designs. The human Aura is comprised of several layers. These are in turn made up of many sub layers. Four of the main layers are of concern to us here.

The *Physical Body Layer* represents the condition of an individual's physical health. Pictures can be found in this layer that represent old traumas to the body.

The *Emotional Body Layer* represents the emotional health of the individual and may contain pictures of stored hurts or unhealthy emotions toward oneself and others.

The *Mental Body Layer* contains pictures of recent thoughts and recent meditations.

The *Karmic Body Layer* represents that which will be drawn to an individual from prearranged agreements made prior to taking the present incarnation, plus any karma created from our thoughts, emotions, and actions.

The four layers that we have mentioned, make up the basic Aura, auric egg, or auric shield. All of these terms are essentially the same and can be used interchangeably.

The auric shield is what separates the energy of the outside world from the being within. The job of the shield is to filter and protect against outside energies that could cause harm to the individual.

It also allows certain karmic energies or lessons to occur for individual growth (see illustration). The lessons that are permitted are encoded within the Aura itself and are generated by thoughts, acts, emotions, and omissions. In other words, this auric shield is like a scorecard that tracks who has done what to whom and who has asked for a similar lesson.

As an example, let's say that you lose your temper and yell at someone for no real reason other than you are tired and cranky. You have just set yourself up for a lesson. Your Aura has now been encoded with a karmic message, "... lesson is needed here."

As previously stated, karma is not a punishment. It is a lesson gathered by your subconscious mind. Just as the subconscious heard and felt the wrong done to the person with whom you were cranky, it will also learn from the experience.

The combination of the pain of your victim and the similar pain you experience when your lesson is completed will help you be more sympathetic in the future, or at least to think before you speak. If you do not learn from that lesson, it will be repeated. So you can see, karma is indeed not a punishment. It is a learning experience.

The Aura also acts to connect you to both the Universal or Cosmic energy and to the energy of Mother Earth.

When the aura is weak, sick, or dirty, it cannot properly filter out the destructive emotions and energies of others from either this plane of existence or another (discarnates). Neither can it properly connect you to the Universal or Earth energies. As a result, you often repeat karmic lessons no longer needed, illness can be more frequent, unhappiness is more common, possession is possible, and a feeling of being lost, disjointed, or not belonging is prevalent.

When the auric shield is weakened, well-meaning and those not so well-meaning friends, relatives, lovers, co-workers, and others can trespass against your shield with raw, uncontrolled energy. Any act directed to you releases some energy into your shield. The energy can be either constructive or destructive. A weak shield cannot defend against the latter nor can it properly channel the former.

The energy referred to may come in the form of love, hate, lust, admiration, etc., and is caught in the auric shield of a dirty and unhealthy Aura. An unhealthy Aura may be rough, sticky, hot, or cold. It may be missing altogether in still other spots. The rips, tears, and holes allow for unwanted visitors such as discarnates. For those unfamiliar with the term, a discarnate is a being that no longer has a body.

There may also be long sticky cords extending into the Aura from people too close to you. These cords can be draining and demanding, thus leaving you without a life or will of your own. Perhaps you have heard of sayings such as "He is tied to mother's apron strings," or "He is riding on so and so's coat-tails," and "He puts me up on a pedestal." These are indications of people who do not have control of their own lives, but are being ruled by another's will and energy. This is known as "giving up your power," and is very unhealthy for the victim.

From well-meaning loved ones to dire enemies, energy follows thought and manifestation follows energy. This is why learning to recognize problems and cleansing the Aura is vital to all practitioners and nonpractitioners of magick alike.

By learning to cleanse the Aura, you learn not only to heal yourself and others, but also to control and shape your energy to your will. Once you control your energy, no one can control you without your permission or knowledge.

Cleansing the Aura

In order to properly cleanse your Aura, you will need to be familiar with a bit of Color Magick. The section in this book on color should help you to select the best color for you. Just so you do not have to turn back and forth if you are unsure, we have listed a few of the basic colors and their properties.

PEARLACEOUS WHITE: Use this color when in doubt. It contains all colors within it and is the favored one of the healing fairies. The use of this color brings them into the home. Healing Fairies can often be seen with the naked eye as dancing balls of colored light. Your first clue that they are in your home is when your cats begin to act as though they are chasing invisible birds.

GOLD: Gold is excellent for building up your energy, especially when it seems to drain too easily. This color represents the energy given by Mother Earth to those in need. The Little People will be around if you use Gold.

SILVER: Silver is used to release pent up energy and blocks. Sometimes when this color is envisioned, it is accompanied by a radiant Black that rests closest to the body while the Silver faces to the outside world. If this happens, you have just set up what is called the "Mirror of Protection." It repels negativity from you and your Aura. When you use Silver to cleanse your Aura, do not be surprised if an old woman comes to you and symbolically destroys your old body and then creates a new one for you from the ashes. She is known as the Crone and is part of the Triple Goddess. You are under her protection when using this color and you may experience magickal initiations when she is present.

DEEP BLUE GREEN: An excellent color to use for emotional upset and release, and for negating deep hurts and other disappointments in life. The Mer people will come with this color, often taking you deep into the realms of the ocean. They are kindly beings who will cleanse your Aura as you shower if you will dedicate the shower head to them. They offer inner calm and peace.

The Cleansing

By now you have reviewed the section on Creative Visualization. If not, please do so and then return to this point. If you are familiar with our method, proceed through the necessary steps to get to your private place.

Once you are safely within your private sanctuary, envision

yourself encased within an egg of light. Begin to explore this egg. How does it look? What color is it? Are there rips, tears, or holes? Is it wet or dry?

These are important questions but do not try to remember them all. Simply explore your auric egg for now and remember that you can always go back later to clean up the problems.

Next envision two trapdoors on swinging hinges, one each at the top and bottom of your Aura. The trapdoor at the bottom has a fine mesh screen over the opening. This screen prevents debris or lower vibrations from entering.

Begin now to see light, the color of your choice for cleansing, swirling up from Mother Earth, pouring up through the trapdoor and through the mesh screen. See this energy rushing up through the bottoms of your feet and slowly moving into the toes, heels and balls of your feet. Up then into the ankles, through the calves to the knees and on upward to the thighs and hips. Follow it upward as it fills your body with a radiant light that glows warmly as it comes into your torso. From the torso feel it spread out into your arms, wrists, hands, and fingers. The warm, beautiful color now courses up the arms to fill your shoulders, neck, face, and head. Feel the energy of the colorful fluid as it pulsates throughout your entire body.

Now see this beautiful liquid filling your auric egg. Up from the Earth, through your body, and spewing from the top of your head, removing all disease, pain, blocks, and foreign energies from the interior of your body. As this energy moves upward, all foreign power cords of a destructive nature immediately dissolve.

Once the Earth energy has filled your auric egg, see all the debris forced out of the trapdoor at the top of your egg. Continue filling the egg until you feel that all debris is gone and all rips, tears, and holes have been mended.

Continue to breathe deeply and slowly. As all the debris is pushed out of the Aura and only the relaxing, healing energy of Mother Earth is left, allow the energy to cleanse the outside of the auric egg; again removing anything attached to it.

Now center yourself within your Aura and the surrounding

energy. At all times you should remain centered. If you are not, continually reposition yourself to remain so. Being off center can interfere with your energy flow and will throw you off balance.

Now you should thank the Mother Earth for what she has provided. You do this by envisioning the Earth encased within a light of glowing green (or whatever color comes to your psyche as being needed). See this light healing the Earth, her flora and fauna, and dissolving the scars human strife has imposed upon her.

This last is important and not only rights your inner and outer world but helps the entire world as a whole. Remember the "Law of Return." Here is how to get a lot of good karmic energy going for you.

Universal or Cosmic Energy/Grounding Yourself

Now try cleansing the Aura in the same fashion as previously described. The only difference is that now you will be using Universal or Cosmic energy instead of Earth energy. Reverse the process by bringing down the energy from the cosmos and let it enter your head and exit at your feet into Mother Earth.

Empowering/Running Energy

Once you are adept at visualizing the two ways to cleanse your Aura, try to run both energies at the same time. See them mixing together within your body and auric egg. Feel them circulating and exiting through their respective trapdoors, taking with them all that does not serve your highest good.

Once you can envision these two powers circulating easily and freely within your body, you have the energy to begin magick. Note that we said that you have the energy to BEGIN magick. Now you must learn to control it and make it grow. This is where the study of the Chakras comes in.

TEST YOUR KNOWLEDGE

THE AURA

MIXED QUIZ

1. The Aura is the energy field surrounding everything animate and inanimate. (True or False)
2. The rips, tears, holes, and cords found in the Aura mean what?
3. The color Silver is used in the Aura to create a shield of protection called the what?
4. The color Gold used in the Aura does what?
5. The process of running energy from the Earth below and the Universe above, into the body is called Empowering. (True or False)

FOR YOUR NOTES

TEST YOUR KNOWLEDGE

ANSWER SHEET

1. True
2. A sure sign of an unhealthy aura that is badly in need of cleansing and healing.
3. The Mirror of Protection.
4. Gold builds up the energy reserves within the body.
5. True

4

The Chakras

The word Chakra is Sanskrit for spinning wheel or vortex. The name was given to these normally invisible energy centers because they resemble spinning wheels or vortexes of colorful, flowing energy.

There are major and minor Chakras throughout the body, along with Nadis or Meridians. These centers and lines are pure energy.

Thoughts, trauma, drugs, and environmental stress can block these energies anywhere from the smallest level, the Nadis/Meridians, to the larger and more health threatening Chakra level. Most people today have one or more blocked Chakras. When properly maintained and balanced, the Chakra's energy maintains proper health, mental ability and power.

The Nadis or Meridians are located at approximately 741 different points throughout the entire body. They constitute a line of electrical energy and are also known as accupressure or acupuncture points.

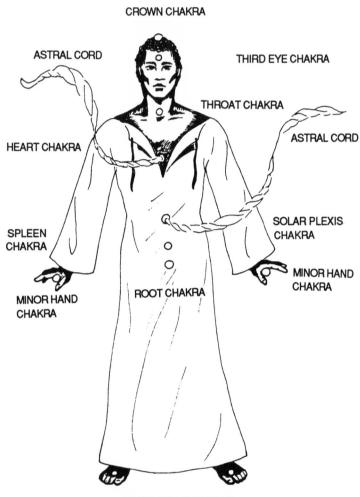

CROWN CHAKRA

ASTRAL CORD

THIRD EYE CHAKRA

THROAT CHAKRA

ASTRAL CORD

HEART CHAKRA

SPLEEN
CHAKRA

SOLAR PLEXIS
CHAKRA

MINOR HAND
CHAKRA

MINOR HAND
CHAKRA

ROOT CHAKRA

MINOR FEET CHAKRAS

The Minor Chakra points of energy are zones where several energy points converge, such as in the palms of the hands or the soles of the feet.

The Major Chakras are located where many points of energy converge and create a major center or vortex of power and energy.

We will be looking at seven Major Chakras in the use and development of magick.

The Chakras, being conductors of energy, are of extreme importance in manifesting what you want onto this plane of existence. Each Chakra, when cleansed and balanced, offers a unique extrasensory ability. If the Chakras are blocked, the energy will not flow properly. The Chakras then can become a hinderance to your magick, thus rendering the outcome unpredictable.

For instance, if your feet and hand Chakras are blocked, you will be incapable of properly imbuing your candle with energy.

The Crown Chakra

The Crown Chakra, located at the top of the head, draws knowledge from the universe, the All Knowing Source. All time is here and now for the practitioner with an unblocked Crown Chakra. The blocking of this Chakra renders you incapable of utilizing this vast knowledge and bars you from joining the Godself to obtain the knowledge of one's own divinity. This center must be in balance if you are to progress both magickally and spiritually. The Crown Chakra's color is Violet.

The Brow Chakra

The Brow Chakra, when blocked, prevents you from seeing on the inner plane. In the child, this Chakra is usually open. Children see auras, secret friends, and fairies. Adults unknowingly close this Chakra when they grow up and are thus limited to the mundane world of vision.

The advantage of having this Chakra open lies in being able to sense future events, to see Auras, and to penetrate into other realms of existence. This second sight is particularly handy if you ever have to call on foreign deities and spirit guides. The ability to see them gives you a distinct advantage over those who cannot. The Brow Chakra's color is Indigo.

Throat Chakra

If you feel a general constriction in your throat most of the time, this is a good indication that your Throat Chakra is blocked. When this happens, any guide or spirit teacher that may have been attracted to you will barely, if ever, get through. What little information that does will be inaccurate at best. Think of yourself as a radio receiver trying to tune in a station. A misaligned receiver will result in poor reception. So it is with your body and this chakra. You must cleanse and tune it for proper perception and reception. The Throat Chakra is the chakra of communication skills. Written, oral, mental, and mediumistic skills are all within the Throat Chakra. The Throat Chakra's color is Blue.

The Heart Chakra

An open Heart Chakra is essential to the seeker of inner wisdom and ancient knowledge. Through this Chakra you meet your inner guides and masters, which are your true teachers. No one can teach you better than they. Others may guide you, as we are doing here, but your true path is unique and can only be discovered within yourself.

The Heart Chakra is also the conduit for the transmission and reception of love. The person who has "hardened their heart" has closed this Chakra. The Heart Chakra's color is Green with Pink.

The Solar Plexus Chakra

Your kinetic energy center and vital to your magick is the Solar Plexus Chakra. This is the center that will aid you in making objects bend or move to your will. Through this center you manifest the vehicle for astral travel. The Chakra must also be in perfect balance and control at all times in order to prevent others from stealing your energy or to prevent you from leaking destructive energy when upset. This leaked energy can turn lights on and off, damage electrical appliances, and move objects.

The Solar Plexus Chakra is the first one attacked by others who wish to gain control over you. These do not have to be other magickians, but unwitting friends, employers, or lovers. They are people to whom you usually cannot say "No." The Solar Plexus Chakra's color is Yellow.

The Spleen Chakra

An unbalanced Spleen Chakra causes individuals to act antisocial. They are unwilling or unable to communicate and relate to others. Poor sexual relations as well as sexual dysfunction are sure signs of a blocked Spleen Chakra.

Self love and identity problems also occur when this center is blocked. This is due to an inability to distinguish between a person's own feelings and emotions, and those of others. Empathy and social interaction are vital traits of a healthy magickian. The Spleen Chakra's color is Orange.

The Root Chakra

The Root Chakra is vital. If it is damaged, blocked or misaligned, you can be in physical peril. It is this Chakra that keeps our bodies functioning and retains us in our present incarnation. The feeling of not wanting to be here (a death wish) is due to a problem with this Chakra. Overly aggressive behavior and paranoia about survival are also good indications of a Root Chakra problem.

For the practitioner of magick, this center is critical for mixing the Earth and Universal energies within the body. It is within this center that the Kundalini or Ancient Dragon lies asleep. This dragon, coiled around the base of the spine, represents the sleeping potential of the Divine Self. Once awakened by working with the Chakras, it slowly rises into all the Chakras, opening each to its full potential and capacity. It is imperative, however, that all blocks and imbalances be cleared or the Kundalini energy will stop at the blocked

Chakra and enhance the problems already there.

Be patient as it may take many lifetimes to achieve the full power of freely flowing energy through each Chakra, the sign of a fully risen Kundalini. This achievement is the highest attainment in magick in the physical body. The Root Chakra's color is Red.

As can be seen in our brief discussion of the Chakras, these centers are the zones that give the ability to exhibit what is erroneously referred to as extrasensory perception. All the exercises endured in ESP laboratories, as far as performing magick is concerned, will not do for you what working with the Chakras will.

The best way to work on the Chakras is while working with the Aura. This can be done every morning upon rising, every night before retiring, or whenever you find time to go to your private place. At the end of this workbook, under resources, we have recommended two tapes that will greatly help you to this end. In their absence, here is a visualization we use to cleanse and balance the Chakras.

Chakra Cleansing and Balancing

After going to your private place and cleansing your Aura, again bring up Earth energy through the lower trapdoor, through your feet and into your body. Let the energy flow upward through your legs and pause at the base of your spine or the Root Chakra.

Imagine the Earth energy cleaning the Root Chakra until the Chakra is a vibrant, glowing Red. Again there will be pictures or symbols that need clearing along with emotions that need healing. Thank them and let them go. You may even find power cords and faces in your Chakras. Again, wash them away. You can visualize this by seeing a soft scrubbing brush breaking free the debris and then letting the energy from Mother Earth act as a hose to wash away all debris from the Chakra. As you work your way upward, eliminate all debris as you did with the Aura cleansing. As with any visualization, choose a technique that is comfortable for you. Try to dissolve cords attached to you but do not attempt to cut them by force.

They will dissolve when you are truly ready to have them gone.

Repeat this process of cleansing and balancing each Chakra with its special color.

SUMMARY

Practitioners of magick who do not understand themselves can hardly hope to understand magick. Above the entrance to many ancient temples of wisdom was a saying, *Initiate Know Thyself.*

Often, this was all the novice practitioner had to go on for many years before the reason behind it was discovered. All magick comes from within, not without. To learn and understand any form of magick, one must understand one's self first, for there is where the real magick lies, asleep and waiting.

In this section of the workbook, we have offered insight into the workings of magick by introducing you to your inner self. From visualization, you have learned the symbols needed to communicate with your magickal self. Backed by strong emotion and desire, you will come to understand the language necessary for manifestation. The cleansing and balancing of the Aura and Chakras frees you from bonds that will keep you a prisoner in a world of helplessness.

Next, we will introduce you to the physical tools necessary for the completion of the magickal act. Combining these mental and physical tools will move you along the road to actually performing Candle Magick.

TEST YOUR KNOWLEDGE

THE CHAKRAS

MIXED QUIZ

1. Chakra is the Sanskrit word for spinning wheel or vortex. (True or False)
2. There are Major and Minor Chakras in the body. (True or False)

3. To see on the inner planes, what Chakra would need to be open?

4. What Chakra would you use to meet your Spirit Guides or Master Teachers?

5. It is just as important to keep the Chakras clean as it is the Aura. (True or False)

FOR YOUR NOTES

TEST YOUR KNOWLEDGE

ANSWER SHEET

1. True
2. True
3. The Brow Chakra gives the astral vision necessary to see beyond what we perceive as reality.
4. The Heart Chakra is where you would meet your Master Teachers and Guides.
5. True

5

Merging Consciousness

In order to better understand why our charts and those in other books specify specific color, oil, herb, fragrance, and bath salt relationships, you should learn how this information is obtained.

Charts outlining these relationships are numerous and, though they vary somewhat from author to author, generally agree on the proper combination for Candle Magick.

Most practitioners of magick, particularly Candle Magick, eventually prefer to tailor each magickal act to a more personal level. In order to do that, you must learn to merge your consciousness with each of the items that you have chosen to formulate your magickal act.

Merging consciousness with an object is not difficult. It is sometimes referred to as mediation, mental imaging, self-hypnosis, or Creative Visualization. Pertinent information about the object's purpose and specific uses can be obtained from the object itself. The images of knowledge obtained by merging with an object are often surprising and can frequently be better relied upon than information found in some books and ancient lore. If this is properly done, you will obtain much of the same information already published or passed down, as image-merging is the source of much information originally. You will, however, be able to obtain some that no one else can obtain because that information is for you alone. No two people receive precisely the same information because no two people and no two objects are exactly alike.

You might begin by gathering together all the items of color, scent, or symbol that our charts have indicated are necessary for a specific magickal goal.

Take these items to a place that is quiet, and at a time that you are least likely to be disturbed. Ground and center yourself within your aura.

Should the item you have first chosen to merge with be a flower, place that flower in the cupped palms of your hands facing toward you. Begin by breathing deeply, inhaling the essence, as you see yourself merging with the consciousness of the flower. Relax. This is not a hurried process but one of enjoyment and relaxation.

Now, use your mental senses to smell, taste, see, hear, and touch each part of the flower. Make a door into each part so that you might fully merge with its inner being. Is the stem hollow? What fragrance is apparent? Do you hear anything? Can you sense the life within the flower? In what form does it reveal itself to you. An elf? Fairy?

When you feel that you have successfully merged with the flower and are in communication with it, ask how it can help you with your magickal act and goal. Is its essence correct for this particular act? Does the color coincide with your needs at this time? Perhaps a different shade might do? By letting your consciousness freely merge, you will obtain your answers.

When you return from merging with the item, be sure to write down everything you have experienced. Pay particular attention to what your senses have revealed. This writing down of perceptions is especially critical as experiences in an altered state of consciousness are rarely retained in memory for long periods and generally fade rapidly. By keeping a journal of all magickal experiences, you can begin to travel further with less effort, and more confidence.

As an example, your first few experiences may glean a little less than accurate information. This is because you may not be allowing yourself the full experience of merging. You must build confidence in your abilities and learn to tune your vibrations to match those of the item you are exploring. After awhile, merging will become second nature to you and your information will be quite accurate.

Perform this merging with each of the items you have chosen. Communicate with each one on an individual basis until you feel that no more information is forthcoming that will aid you at the time. Then gather all the items together and perform a united merging to build harmony between the items and yourself. Every little factor in a magickal act counts. The more of yourself you put into it, the stronger your magick will be.

Correlation by Astrology

Another excellent method for discovering the proper correlations in magick is to become familiar with astrology. As each particular culture has its own variation of basic astrology, find one that feels "right" for you. Use its attributes and correlations for your magick.

An excellent work entitled *Culpepper's Color Herbal*, edited by David Potterton, exemplifies, from a healing aspect, the Zodiacal correlations of herbs. First published by Nicholas Culpepper in 1649, it is still considered an early definitive work on the astrological correlation of herbs.

TEST YOUR KNOWLEDGE

MERGING CONSCIOUSNESS

MIXED QUIZ

1. The merging of your consciousness with an object is impossible. (True or False)
2. Difficulty in merging may possibly mean that your chakras need cleansing. (True or False)

3. Try merging with a crystal. Record your findings.
4. Try merging with a plant. Record your findings.
5. Try merging with an animal. Record your findings.

FOR YOUR NOTES

TEST YOUR KNOWLEDGE

ANSWER SHEET

1. False—The sense of merging comes from the Heart and Spleen Chakras. If you experience difficulty in merging, clean these Chakras.
2. True
3. Exercise—Self explanatory.
4. Exercise—Self explanatory.
5. Exercise—Self explanatory.

PART FIVE

Life begets life. Energy creates energy. It is by spending
ourselves that one becomes rich.

—Sarah Bernhardt (1844–1923)

1

The Effective Use of Color

COLOR

We live in a sea of living energy. Our conscious mind per-
ceives, in the form of color, only a fragment of this living
energy. Our subconscious, however, misses nothing, and, as
psychologists are finding, these color radiations have a
tremendous influence upon our health, thoughts, and actions.

A major tool in magick is the proper use of color to one's
best advantage. In dress, decor, or healing, color is of the
utmost importance for one's success.

Knowing what a color can do on a conscious, as well as a
subconscious level, is what Candle Magick is all about. The
following pages will introduce you to thirteen different colors.

White

A pastel combination of all colors, White reflects light with
little to no absorption. Whenever in doubt in a magickal act,

use White, which is the most highly balanced form of spirituality possible. White contains virtues in their highest form, and is therefore very protective. It is beyond the word or term God/dess. It is the Creative Source itself, zero, the alpha, the light from which all life springs, the female aspect of God, the Craft of the Wise, the full of the moon, the symbol of the life giving Mother, and all female mysteries.

ASSOCIATIONS
Planet: Moon
Day: Monday
Hours: 1st/8th/15th/22nd
Energy: Female
Color: Silvers/Pearls/Creams/Grays/Iridescent Whites
               (Pale Pinks, Violets, Blue hues, etc.)

KEY PHRASES
To seem unreachable, untouchable, incorruptible; to repel destructive energies; to raise vibrations; to heal emotions, births, rapes, children, and pets; to build purity, balance the aura, confound enemies, create illusions, and contact spirit helpers.

Black

An intense concentration of all colors, it absorbs light. Unlike other colors, Black reflects very little, if any, light back to the viewer. This can give the false impression that Black is the absence of color. It is actually the absence of color reflection. Think of this color as a black hole in space. It absorbs all light with little or no reflection back, thus it becomes a receptacle or a transporter for all that you do not need or want.

Properly used, Black can be one of the most useful and powerful colors available. However, misused, it can cause disaster.

ASSOCIATIONS
Planet: Saturn
Day: Saturday

    Hours: 1st/8th/15th/22nd
    Energy: Female
    Color: Dark Blues, Black, Dark Browns,
              and most dark colors

KEY PHRASES
To absorb or remove anything; to end something; to remove or encase undesirable energies; to break up a blocked or stagnant situation. The great mystery solver. The Crone, the Unconscious.

Brown

Earth energy. It is feminine in its nature and related to its sisters the Moon and Saturn. Being a relatively balanced combination of Red, Yellow, and Blue, depending on the intensity level, it can be used successfully on Monday, Friday, or Saturday. Brown is one of the more complex colors, with varied associations.

ASSOCIATIONS
    Planet: Moon (Tan Browns)/Venus (all)/Saturn
              (Dark Browns)
    Day: Monday/Friday/Saturday
    Hour: 1st/8th/15th/22nd
    Energy: Female
    Color: Browns, earth tones

KEY PHRASES
To acquire basic material needs for survival; to learn to ground and center your consciousness with the earth; to obtain money that is not transient by working with your hands, i.e. laborer, farmer, gardener, etc.; to attune with trees (red-browns) and communicate with their intelligence.

Gray

This color is unique, due to its aspect of neutrality. Gray can be used to neutralize anything from a magickal act that no longer serves your best interest, to the neutralization of destructive energies in a passive, non-karmic fashion. It is a perfect balance of Black and White, and therefore absorbs and repels. With this quality, Gray draws in the undesirable energies and then sends them out to the universe for dispersal as neither destructive nor constructive properties.

ASSOCIATIONS

Planet:	Moon
Day:	Monday
Hours:	1st/8th/15th/22nd
Energy:	Female and Male
Color:	Gray

KEY PHRASES

To erase, cancel, neutralize, and return to the universe without repercussion; to eradicate or jumble destructive forces; to attract neither destructive nor constructive energies to your life (this includes people and situations).

Blue

Blue transforms violence, anger, and hate. It soothes and cools. It gives peace, calm, harmony, satisfaction, bliss, oneness, and understanding of the spiritual realms. It is predominantly feminine energy, and is ruled by either the Moon, Venus, or Saturn, depending on the hue. However, many consider the Royal Blues as belonging to the expansive male energies or Jupiter. Therefore, it is left for the student, to experiment and decide for him- or herself which works best.

ASSOCIATIONS

Planet:	Moon, Venus, Saturn, Jupiter
Day:	Monday, Friday, Saturday, Thursday
Hours:	1st/8th/15th/22nd
Energy:	Female (sometimes Male when used with Jupiter/ Thursday)
Colors:	Blue Whites/Moon, Blues/Venus, Dark Blues/Saturn, Royal Blue/Jupiter

KEY PHRASES

Religious beliefs in a pure and healthy state, inner calm, peace from within, first contact with Higher Self, spiritual well being, wisdom, truth and light, dedication, and loyalty.

Yellow

Yellow is a color of mental clarity, swiftness, and accuracy. A sunny, positive disposition with spiritual attuning to the healing forces of male energy (refer to Gold).

ASSOCIATIONS

Planet:	Mercury
Day:	Wednesday
Hours:	1st/8th/15th/22nd
Energy:	Male
Colors:	Yellow

KEY PHRASES

To obtain knowledge; to learn swiftly; to gain insight into problems. Yellow represents all institutions of learning, particularly upper level studies (especially in sciences). Alters dark mental mood swings. Enhances the knowledge of healing, the ability to concentrate, and the retention of memory. Yellow attracts people, as it has a warm compelling energy, and can also be used to compel another to do your bidding.

Gold

The male half of the Cosmic or Universal Life Force—sun energy. Intelligent action or action motivated by deliberation and knowledge, usually with healing, money, or wealth in mind. Gold is related to Orange and Yellow, in that it is a higher vibration of these two colors, and any one of the three can actually be used on Sunday (Sun) with success. The choice here is for the student to experiment, and then decide which color best suits his or her needs. Generally speaking, Orange vibrates to physical and mental action, while Yellow vibrates to mental action only (better attributed to Wednesday/Mercury). Lastly, Gold would be indicative of intelligent, quick action, with a monetary emphasis.

ASSOCIATIONS
  Planet: Sun
  Day: Sunday
  Hours: 1st/8th/15th/22nd
  Energy: Male (Amazon Female)
  Colors: Gold

KEY PHRASES

To attract money and power (you constantly will have to work to keep it however); to heal and rejuvenate your being; to attract happy, active people to your life. Gold imparts the energy and intelligence to take proper action in a monetary situation. Attracts stock market gains, transient abundance, the appearance of wealth and grandeur. Epitomizes the gambler, the risk taker; chasing a pot of gold at the end of an elusive rainbow. It expedites money you know is coming but has not yet arrived due to red tape, lawsuits, etc.

Red

Red is a fiery color that attracts and magnetizes, but must be used with discernment to avoid disastrous results. The shade of Red used or considered in your magickal act will be of extreme importance here. Stay with the lighter, brighter shades of Red and leave the darker shades for the more experienced practitioners for now. The darker shades are for wars, battles, blood, hate, and danger.

ASSOCIATIONS
  Planet: Mars
  Day: Tuesday
  Hours: 1st/8th/15th/22nd
  Energy: Male (Amazon Female)
  Colors: Red

KEY PHRASES

Lust, physical desire, anger, base energy, war, blood, pain, attracts and magnetizes, courage, enemies, danger. Red stimulates and energizes. Cherry-Reds are for physical and mental lovemaking, but without the brutal force of the darker hues.

Pink

Pink is a lighter shade of Red. It deals with a spiritual, emotional love rather than the physical form. Pink represents love that comes from the heart that is freely given without condition, such as the emotions and feelings between parent and child, close friends, or family.

ASSOCIATIONS
  Planet: Venus
  Day: Friday
  Hours: 1st/8th/15th/22nd
  Energy: Female
  Colors: Pink

KEY PHRASES
Love from the heart without the sexual connotation, purest form of love, raises vibrations, love without selfishness, feminine, spiritual healing, banish lower vibrations and hate, love of friends and family, affections, unselfish emotions, to start a relationship.

Orange

Orange is a combination of Yellow/Mercury/mental agility and Red/Mars/action-energy. Thus you have the best of both worlds, the energies and actions of Red, yet the intelligence to know how to use this action. The overaggressive nature of the color Red/Mars is now toned and tapered with the healing wisdom rays of Yellow/Mercury that nurtures the entire system. Sunday is the best day for the use of the color Orange. It can be used on Tuesday or Wednesday with success, depending on your magickal goals. If used on Tuesday, the emphasis is on physical action. If used on Wednesday, it is on mental action whereas Sunday is a balance of both.

ASSOCIATIONS
  Planet: Sun/Mars/Mercury
  Day: Sunday/Tuesday/Wednesday

Hours: 1st/8th/15th/22nd
Energy: Male (Amazon Female)
Colors: Orange, rarely Red, sometimes Yellow

KEY PHRASES
Prosperity, energy building, attracts others in a positive
way, attracts success, good luck and fortune. Builds vitality,
energy, and stamina. Encourages fun and discourages laziness. Enhances mental agility, accompanied by the ability to
take physical action toward a desired goal. Energizes the
entire system. Promotes a happy-go-lucky appearance.

Green

Green really does bring the luck of the Irish, but in cases of
money, you could be chasing rainbows. Money sought with
this color seems to fade quickly and trickle in a little at a time,
just enough to whet your appetite (refer to Gold or Brown).
Think of Green as being an elusive leprechaun and you will
better understand what I mean. Green stimulates growth,
especially concerning your garden and communication with
plant life or garden fairies. Green is an Earth color, and is
used on Friday. Depending upon the magickal system you
employ, it may be used on Wednesday, as Wednesday is also
used for healing. Green used on Friday gives an emotional
healing (matters of the heart), while Wednesday emphasizes
healing knowledge.

ASSOCIATIONS
Planet: Venus/Mercury
Day: Friday/Wednesday
Hours: 1st/8th/15th/22nd
Energy: Female or Male
Colors: Green

KEY PHRASES
Money, healing, fertility, good luck and fortune. Attracts
success. Communication with the plant kingdom (darker
Greens) or fairies (pastels). The secrets of healing are yours
when you tune in to this color. Use in conjunction with herbal
healing techniques.

Purple

Purple is the color of expansion in all forms. If you want to do something in a big way, this is the color to use. Purple expands anything you desire, i.e., spirituality, business, money, health, or love. The Royal Blues are less expansive, dealing more with the emotional and spiritual levels of Jupiter. Therefore, the Royal or Dark Blues are often attributed to Saturn.

A word of caution, however: if you do not already have the items of your desire, do not use Jupiter. Jupiter only expands and brings more of what you already have. To obtain the items of your desires, use Sun/Sunday/Orange in order to manifest what you currently do not have in your life.

ASSOCIATIONS
Planet:	Jupiter
Day:	Thursday
Hours:	1st/8th/15th/22nd
Energy:	Male
Colors:	Purple, sometimes Royal Blue, Dark Purple/Saturn

KEY PHRASES

Money begets money, the rich get richer; poverty begets poverty, the poor get poorer. Purple brings more of what you already have, in a bigger way. Wisdom, high idealism, knowledge of the higher realms of magick, spiritual protection and healing, the becoming of your highest potential, becoming your God/dess self, reversal of a jinxed condition. Manipulation of law, business, commerce, courts, judges, people in a position of power over you. Enhancement of power, psychic ability, male energy. Influence older men of power and women with a strong male nature. Protective energy, bestows fame, power, and recognition in a chosen field. Progressive energies that continually expand and build.

TEST YOUR KNOWLEDGE

COLOR

MIXED QUIZ

1. What color would you use to represent Mars?
2. What color would you use to represent the Sun?
3. Black comes under the rulership of Monday.
   (True or False)
4. Pastels and whites represent what planet?
5. What color would you use for transforming violence, anger, and hate?

FOR YOUR NOTES

TEST YOUR KNOWLEDGE

ANSWER SHEET

1. Red(s)
2. Orange(s)
3. False—Saturday
4. Moon
5. Blue(s)

2

The Effective Use of Fragrance

We have already discussed in some depth the importance of carefully aligning your magickal acts. Once set in motion, they achieve your magickal goal. This process has been called the domino effect, as each act represents one domino leading to your ultimate desire. As important as selecting the proper color is the proper use of fragrance and the taking of a ritual bath.

The terms oil and fragrance are used interchangeably throughout this section. Fragrance, in the form of oil, forms the basis for most scents found in floor washes, sprays, bath salts, and incenses. Generally the name of the oil or combination of oils is attached as a fragrance identifier to the base product. i.e., Sandlewood Bath Salts.

Fragrance affects the central nervous system, as well as the auric field of the body. A fragrance can alleviate depressive moods by raising bodily vibrations, or can have the opposite effect by lowering bodily vibrations.

By arranging these essential fragrances into special combinations, you will find your will and desire multiplied, adding more of the essential dominoes for a proper magical act. We would, however, encourage the new practitioner to use only pure oils without mixing them into combinations until becoming more familiar with their individual properties and powers. Most of the higher vibrational fragrances consist of various combinations of Sandlewood, Myrrh, Frankincense, Cinnamon, Patchouly, and Symatra Benzoin. This is why several fragrances claim similar capabilities but are marketed with varying names.

One formula may use Cinnamon, Benzoin, Frankincense and Myrrh. Another, Cinnamon, Spices, and Sandlewood. Nevertheless, these are generally the basic fragrances that make up the higher vibrational oils.

Since fragrance combinations can greatly enhance your Candle Magick, it is important that you understanding something about properly combining them.

All fragrances have astrological attributes and are thus assigned a ruling planet that indicates the fragrance's virtues. These virtues are combined with the proper day, hour, moon phase, etc., to obtain the maximum benefit. The combinations are used to create everything from basic bath salts to candles for use in Advanced Candle Magick that are highly charged and incredibly potent.

The creation of fragrances can be a difficult process. There are many good books available on the market today if you are inclined to spend the time it takes to develop pure scents.

For those of you without the time or facilities to create your own fragrances, pure essential oils can be found both singly and in basic astrological combinations at most occult supply stores. They are labeled under various titles such as Protection Oil, Pleasant Dreams or Goddess Oil, etc. Oils such as Commanding, Controlling, Compelling, and High Joan/John the Conqueror, are used to intensify your will.

Most quality essential oils, i.e., those that are pure and not diluted, are rather expensive, particularly if they have been made to magickal standards. There are, however, many less expensive oils, sometimes diluted, that are easy to obtain. These are okay to use but they are less potent and less fragrant and will require more of your concentration to properly energize them with your purpose and will at the appropriate time. So if your budget is limited, use the cheaper oils but be prepared to spend more effort with them.

If you do purchase the expensive oils but wish to dilute them for whatever reason, many of them can be cut by fifty percent or more with a Virgin Olive Oil, Palm Oil, or a similar quality bulk oil. Be sure to inquire from whom you purchase the oil if, in fact, it can be cut further and with what compatible oils to cut it.

TABLE 1
FRAGRANCE ASSOCIATIONS

MONDAY/MOON/WHITES/EMOTIONS
White Rose, White Garden Lily, or Gardenia
TUESDAY/MARS/REDS/AGGRESSION
Pine, Carnation, or Honeysuckle
WEDNESDAY/MERCURY/YELLOWS/MENTAL
Lily of the Valley, Lavender, or Bayberry
THURSDAY/JUPITER/PURPLES/EXPANSION
Magnolia, Sandlewood, or Sage
FRIDAY/VENUS/GREENS/LOVE
Primrose, Thyme, or Lilac
SATURDAY/SATURN/BLACKS/ENDINGS
Water Violets, Black Orchid, or Hyacinth
SUNDAY/SUN/ORANGES/CREATING
Rosemary, Rue, or Cloves

NOTE: It is your option in which form to use these fragrances, either as an herb, flower, perfume, oil, incense, or bath salts.

TABLE 2
FRAGRANCES RULED BY THE MOON

Balm
Coconut
Eucalyptus

Gardenia
Jasmine
Lily
Lotus
Myrrh
Poppy
Sandalwood
Water Lily
Wintergreen

TABLE 3
FRAGRANCES RULED BY MARS

All Spice
Carnation
Dragon's Blood
Ginger
High John the Conqueror
Honeysuckle
Hot Peppers
Peppermint
Pine
Snapdragon

TABLE 4
FRAGRANCES RULED BY MERCURY

Azalea
Bayberry
Clover
Fern
Lavender
Lemon Grass
Lily of the Valley
Mandrake
Peppermint
Hemp
Tobacco

TABLE 5

FRAGRANCES RULED BY JUPITER

Anise
Datura
Lime
Magnolia
Maple
Meadowsweet
Nutmeg
Oak
Sage
Sandalwood

TABLE 6

FRAGRANCES RULED BY VENUS

Adam and Eve
African Violet
Cherry
Lilac
Primrose
Rose
Spearmint
Strawberry
Thyme
Vanilla

TABLE 7

FRAGRANCES RULED BY SATURN

Black Orchid
Hyacinth
Iris

Morning Glory
Opium Poppy
Pansy
Patchouly
Peyote
Solomon's Seal
Water Violets

TABLE 8

FRAGRANCES RULED BY THE SUN

Cedar
Cloves
Chrysanthemum
Cinnamon
Frankincense
Juniper
Marigold
Rosemary
Rowan
Rue

TEST YOUR KNOWLEDGE

FRAGRANCE

MIXED QUIZ

1. Fragrance affects the olfactory sense and the central nervous system. (True or False)
2. Fragrance does not affect the auric vibration. (True or False)
3. The oil, Carnation, is used for what planet?
4. What fragrance could you use to stimulate mental agility?
5. Bath salts, floor washes, and herbal and floral sprays do not have the same affect upon the body and aura as pure essential oils do. (True or False)

FOR YOUR NOTES

TEST YOUR KNOWLEDGE

ANSWER SHEET

1. True
2. False—Fragrance can raise or lower the vibration rate of the Aura.
3. Mars.
4. Under Mercury, Lily of the Valley, Lavender and Bayberry are listed.
5. This answer is both true and false. It would depend on whether or not the items had a pure essential base.

3

The Magickal Bath

The magickal bath is an excellent way to prepare your mind and body for any magickal act. The very action of choosing the related perfume, oil, or scent for your bath begins to prepare and program your subconscious for what is ahead.

Bath salts help to keep you grounded and centered in your work while being protective as well.

The actual bath itself uplifts and enhances the mind, body, and energy (auric) field surrounding you. It also clears from the aura unwanted or inharmonious influences that may hinder your work.

During the magickal bath is an opportune time to clearly see what it is you are wishing to create or to release back into the universe. Above all, it is a time to cleanse, relax, empower, and meditate upon what you are about to manifest.

How to Prepare the Magickal Bath

1. Pour water into the freshly cleaned tub. (It does no good to be taking a cleansing bath in a dirty tub.)
2. Place the selected perfume, oil, herb, etc., into the tub. Food coloring may be added to intensify the directional energies used.
3. Add a tablespoon of sea salt or Epsom salts to the water.
4. Now place both hands over the water and envision what it is you want the bath to do for you. Formulate this clearly in your mind and state three times what you want.
5. Visualize beams of light from above you, entering your head, and below you, entering your feet. Now visualize these colored lights circulating in and around your body and emerging from your hands into the water. When you can see the tub of water (in your mind's eye) explode with light or color, you know your bath is properly charged.
6. To do magick, one must maintain the protective Aura:
   a. Sit in the tub and imagine that you are encased within a protective egg of shining silver light.
   b. As you breathe in, everything you need to successfully complete your magick is being drawn in from the universe around you.
   c. Visualize this energy entering from the top of your head and the bottom of your spine.
   d. Picture it circulating within the auric egg, cleaning away debris.
   e. As you exhale, everything you do not need (debris) is being released from the Aura into neutral energy.
   f. Once you can visualize a clean Aura and the energies are flowing freely down from the Universe and up from the Earth, center your consciousness.
   g. Center your consciousness in your heart. Visualize that this center glows and radiates throughout your aura.
   h. As you exit your bath, you are now prepared to undertake any magickal act.

This last step is what will protect you and keep you safely grounded to Earth while keeping you attached to the Life Source. By centering your consciousness in your heart, you will do all magick with compassion and love. Never neglect your Aura; it is the key to *all magick* and is your protective shield.

Should you find one or more of the above steps difficult, consider that you may be too tired or have an error somewhere. Often the Creative Visualization process will be impaired if all is not correct for the desired magickal act. Retrace your steps and look over your worksheet for possible errors.

TEST YOUR KNOWLEDGE

THE MAGICKAL BATH

MIXED QUIZ

1. The magickal bath is an excellent way to prepare your mind and body for any magickal act.
2. The act of choosing a fragrance for your magickal bath begins to prepare your subconscious for the Candle Magick ahead. (True or False)
3. Bath salts do what to you in relation to your magick?
4. The actual bath cleans the body but not the auric field. (True or False)
5. The magickal bath is the time to relax and allow your mind to drift away from all worries, giving no thought to the magick you are about to perform. (True or False)

FOR YOUR NOTES

TEST YOUR KNOWLEDGE

ANSWER SHEET

1. True
2. True
3. Bath salts help to keep you grounded and centered in your work while being well protects.
4. False—The actual bath itself uplifts and enhances the mind, body, and energy (auric) field.
5. False—During the bath is an opportune time to clearly see what it is you are wishing to create or release back into the universe. Above all, it is a time to cleanse, relax, empower, and meditate upon what you are about to manifest.

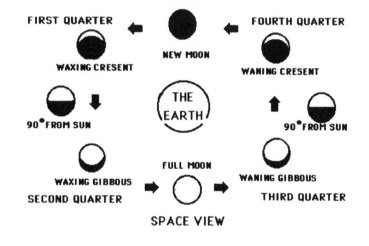

FIRST QUARTER ← NEW MOON ← FOURTH QUARTER

WAXING CRESENT   WANING CRESENT

THE EARTH

90° FROM SUN   90° FROM SUN

WAXING GIBBOUS   FULL MOON   WANING GIBBOUS

SECOND QUARTER   THIRD QUARTER

SPACE VIEW

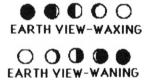

EARTH VIEW—WAXING

EARTH VIEW—WANING

PART SIX

I think that wherever your journey takes you, there are new gods waiting there, with devine patience and laughter.

—Susan M. Watkins, born 1945

1

The Cycles of the Moon

The Moon has a dramatic influence on humans, animals, and plants. This influence causes the tides to rise and fall, and raises and lowers the sap and essential juices in trees and plants. It also is believed to cause strange behavior in humans and animals, thus the term "lunatic" was coined. Knowing how to best utilize the Moon's influence will assist you in the potency and efficiency of your Candle Magick work.

MOON CYCLE

In order to simplify a rather complex subject, suffice it to say that the Moon has two cycles, and three phases during each cycle.

The Waxing Cycle

The waxing cycle of the Moon is the period from new Moon to full Moon. Waxing cycle magick is used to begin new projects, expand, grow, prosper, protect, and raise vibrations for

113

enhanced spirituality and knowledge. Providing a shield of
protection for yourself and loved ones is best done on a waxing Moon. Use the waxing cycle also to create love, harmony,
and peace at home, and for that long deserved promotion.
Begin your magick on the new Moon and conclude on the full
Moon, or until your candle burns out.

New Moon:	Entire Moon appears dark. Sun and Moon in conjunction.
Waxing Crescent:	Light crescent on right side of Moon.
First Quarter:	The right half of the Moon is lit (ninety degrees from sun, end of first quarter, beginning of second quarter).
Waxing Gibbous:	Three-fourths of the Moon is now lit.
Full Moon:	Entire Moon is lit. Moon and Sun in Opposition.

The Waning Cycle

The waning cycle of the Moon is the period from the Full
Moon to the New Moon. Waning cycle magick is best for dissolving disease and destructive energy. Use this time for
diminishing influences you no longer need or want in your
life. Remove lower vibrations from your house and work
place. Neutralize hostile situations, conditions, and memories.
Release them for the betterment of your mental health. Begin
your magick on the full Moon and conclude on the New
Moon, or until the candle burns out.

Full Moon:	Entire Moon appears lit. Sun and Moon in opposition.
Waning Crescent:	Dark crescent appears on right side of Moon (disseminating).
Third Quarter:	The right half of the Moon is now dark (ninety degrees from sun, end of third quarter, beginning of fourth quarter).
Waning Gibbous:	Three-fourths of the Moon is now dark (Balsomic).
New Moon:	Entire Moon appears dark. Sun and Moon in conjunction.

TEST YOUR KNOWLEDGE

CYCLES OF THE MOON

MIXED QUIZ

1. The same effect that causes the tides to rise and fall affects magickal energy. (True or False)
2. Name the two major Moon cycles.
3. To bring something to you or to manifest something, which Moon cycle would you normally use?
4. To send something away from you or to dissolve something, which Moon cycle would you normally use?
5. If the right quarter of the Moon is lit, it is a waxing Moon. (True or False)

FOR YOUR NOTES

TEST YOUR KNOWLEDGE

ANSWER SHEET

1. True
2. Waxing and waning
3. Waxing cycle
4. Waning cycle
5. True

2

The Days of the Week and Their Planetary Correspondences

Each day of the week has a signature, an energy that creates the illusion of a personality. Therefore, a day of the week, with the same traits as those of a particular planet, has been dedicated to that planet.

If you learn the traits of the planet, you then understand the energy pertaining to that particular day of the week. Of course, the reverse would also be true. This will help you to match up your desires with the proper traits for the days of the week and to choose the correct corresponding planet. All of these traits must be properly understood and utilized for the best results in your magick.

Everything that exists has a dual nature. Nothing can exist in purely the male (positive) or female (negative) state. For all male energy, there is equal and opposite female energy.

Conversely, for the female energy, there is also the male counterpart.

This is an important aspect, as you will find yourself drawn to either male or female energies. It is rare for the magickal practitioner to use equal male and female energies, as few of us are in perfect harmony and balance. Any of the three ways is useful, but the ideal is a perfect balance of both the male and female energies.

A word of caution is warranted here. *Do not confuse gender with positive (male) and negative (female) energy currents.* These are more terms than *gender*, descriptions. It is natural in our current society for a male figure to be used for Martian energies and a female figure for Venus. However, due to the overabundance of male energy now influencing our planet, many groups are using the female side of Mars. This is just as valid as using the male side of Venus. Remember, everything has a dual nature. So, if one day of the week states it has strong male or female energy, know that it is stating energy, not gender. A man with strong Venus energies would be an unaggressive male, an artist, a poet; he might be either gay or heterosexual. A Mars or Martian female would be dynamic, aggressive, and could also be either gay or heterosexual.

DAYS OF THE WEEK

MONDAY
RULED BY THE MOON/Silvers, Grays, Creams, Whites
RULES/emotions, protection, healing, women's mysteries

TUESDAY
RULED BY MARS/Reds of all shades
RULES/conqueror, power over enemies

WEDNESDAY
RULED BY MERCURY/Yellows
RULES/healings mental

THURSDAY
RULED BY JUPITER/Royal Purple and Royal Blue
RULES/growth, expansion, generosity

FRIDAY
RULED BY VENUS/Greens, Pinks, Pastels
RULES/lovers and pleasure, affairs of the heart

SATURDAY
RULED BY SATURN/Blacks, Dark purples, and Blues
RULES/obstacles, to give or break, to overcome a block

SUNDAY
RULED BY THE SUN/Orange, Yellows, and Golds
RULES/health, prosperity, leadership, joy, protection

TEST YOUR KNOWLEDGE

DAYS OF THE WEEK

TRUE OR FALSE

1. Each of the planets in our solar system has traits that are like a personality. Anything that has similar traits is placed under the rulership of one of these planets. (True or False)
2. Each day of the week is ruled by a specific planet. (True or False)
3. Tuesday is ruled by what planet?
4. Friday is ruled by what planet?
5. Saturday is ruled by what planet?

FOR YOUR NOTES

TEST YOUR KNOWLEDGE

ANSWER SHEET

1. True
2. True
3. Mars
4. Venus
5. Saturn

3

The Hour of the Magickian

The method of timekeeping to be used for your magickal work will not be based on your wristwatch time (midnight to midnight) but on the Sun's rising time. This method of timekeeping dates back to ancient Greece and is referred to here as the "Magickian's Time."

The times for sunrise and sunset will vary with your location on the planet. An individual located away from the equator will have a much different time sequence or perspective from that of someone located directly on the equator. Our best advice is to check with an ephemeris, newspaper, fisherman's guide, or almanac for local times of sunrise and sunset.

Currently, we use a system of accounting for time that recognizes twenty-four hours within one solar day, or one rotation of the Earth on its axis. Although each day may go slightly over or under this period by several seconds or minutes, the average solar day is twenty-four hours long.

As an example, if the Sun rises in your area at 6:00 A.M.,

then what time would it be if you were using Magickian's Time? Right! It would be 0:00 o'clock. This is the *beginning of the day* and the *beginning of the first hour.* Anytime between 0:00 and 0:59:59 is considered the first hour after sunrise. When 7:00 A.M. comes around, it would be 1:00 or the *beginning of the second hour* after sunrise. Each hour after sunrise would then be numbered and counted consecutively (1–24) until the Sun rose the next day. Since it is easy to confuse 3:00 A.M. with 3:00 P.M., this 1–24 hour method was devised to alleviate the confusion. Therefore the magickian's day is considered to be from sunrise to sunrise.

As an example, if the Sun rose at 6:00 A.M., the first hour would be for the next sixty minutes. At 7:00 A.M., Magickian's Time would be 1:00 or the beginning of the second hour. This method would continue until approximately 6:00 A.M. the next morning, or the end of the twenty-fourth hour, which is also the beginning of the first hour of the next day. Remember, the sunrise to sunrise period does not always start exactly on the hour as our example shows. Sunrise may be at 6:31 A.M. so 1:00 Magickian's Time would be at 7:31 A.M., regular time.

Not a very hard thing to understand but it takes a bit of getting used to. Since man is basically a daytime, lazy creature, you can see why the present time system we use is more convenient. It is much easier to refer to a wristwatch that keeps time on an unvarying, twenty-four hour day even if the system is inaccurate and must be adjusted periodically. Since you are a magickian and magickians are not known for their laziness, all times on the charts in this workbook will be Magickian's Time.

Begin by reviewing the two charts marked ''Table of Day Hours'' (page 176) and ''Table of Evening Hours'' (page 177). Once you know the time the Sun rises in your area, look to the tables. For one hour, or sixty minutes after the Sun rises, it will be considered your first hour of that day.

Now look at the days of the week under their respective first hours. Notice anything similar? Each day of the week, within its perspective first hour, is ruled by itself. In other words, Sunday, during its first hour after sunrise, is ruled by the Sun; Monday is ruled by the Moon, and so forth throughout the week. Note that this pattern is repeated for the eighth, fifteenth, and twenty-second hours. Two hours later at the next sunrise, the next ruling planet takes over and begins its ruling cycle.

So how does this relate to using your workbook and producing your magickal act? Since you now know the difference between a waxing and a waning Moon and how it will relate to your work, combine this knowledge with the correct day of the week and the correct hour of the day to further enhance your magick and align one more magickal domino.

Mixing and Matching Your Work

Once you feel comfortable using the Tables of Day and Evening Hours, refer to the Mixing and Matching Table on page 174. This advanced table is read just as you would read the other tables, but with one slight difference. Instead of symbols representing the pure planetary hours, you now have attributes.

The Mixing and Matching table was created to help you understand the key meanings and relationships between the various days of the week and their respective planetary hours.

Since we cannot always perform Candle Magick at the ideal times, we must therefore consider alternatives.

For example, find Monday on the table and locate the hour of the Moon. One of the attributes is "Women's Mysteries." Now look at Friday. Locate the hour of Mercury. The key attribute here is "Love with Wisdom." The day is what is of primary importance while the hours are secondary. Thus on Wednesday, the hour of Venus displays the attribute "Wisdom in Love." These differences are subtle but very real and important when performing Candle Magick.

MEANING OF PLANETARY HOURS

Moon: Monday
Associations: Subconscious, healing, emotions, love, spirituality healing wounds, children, small animals, women's mysteries, the female side of men, mothers, sisters, female partners, wives, instincts.

Identity: Female (males that identify with their female natures).
Color: Silvers, Gray, Creams, Pinks, Pastels.
Fragrance: Jasmine, White Garden Lily, or Gardenia.

Mars: Tuesday
Associations: War, lust, violence, fast action, victory over enemies, strength, endurance, leadership, soldiers, independence, Amazon women, military strategy and all competitions of a physical nature.
Identity: Male
Color: Reds, Oranges, and Red colors.
Fragrance: Pine, Carnation, or Honeysuckle.

Mercury: Wednesday
Associations: Mental, learning, higher education, groups and group strategy. Addictions, communications, travel, young people, messages, perception, self expression, artist, Bard, poet, and writer.
Identity: Male
Color: Yellows primarily.
Fragrance: Lily of the Valley, Lavender, or Bayberry.

Jupiter: Thursday
Associations: Growth, expansion, prosperity, money, business, attracts more of what you have. Men in professions, older men with a generous nature. Women in professions identifying with their male nature.
Identity: Male
Color: Purples and sometimes Royal Blue.
Fragrance: Magnolia, Sandalwood, or Sage.

Venus: Friday
Associations: Love, peace, beauty, gentleness, women's problems, healing, protection, lovers, ease, pleasure, affairs.
Identity: Female
Color: Greens, Pinks, Pastel Blue.
Fragrance: Primrose, Thyme, or Lilac.

Saturn: Saturday
Associations: Limitations, the elderly, endings, deaths, blocks,

constrictions, and those restricting you.
Identity: Female
Color: Blacks, dark colors.
Fragrance: Violets, Black Orchid, or Hyacinth.

Sun: Sunday
Associations: Happiness, prosperity, joy, healing, protection, power, leadership, ego, authority figure, fathers, husbands.
Identity: Male
Color: Orange, Yellow, Gold.
Fragrance: Rosemary, Rue or Cloves.

Remember that although each planet may say male or female dominant, this should not deter you from using a male planet for a woman, or a female planet for a man. The reason for this is that all beings are a combination of both male and female energies. (Review Days of the Week.)

TEST YOUR KNOWLEDGE

HOUR OF THE MAGICKIAN

TRUE OR FALSE

1. We currently use a method of time keeping that recognizes twenty-four hours in each solar day. This method is slightly inaccurate but convenient to use.
2. Our current method of time keeping runs from midnight to midnight.
3. The time used by magickians runs from sunrise to sunrise instead of midnight to midnight.
4. If the sun rose at 5:00 A.M. on Thursday and your wristwatch now reads 5:45 A.M., you are within the first magickal hour.
5. Each day of the week during the first magickal hour is ruled by its primary planet.

FOR YOUR NOTES

TEST YOUR KNOWLEDGE

ANSWER SHEET

1. True
2. True
3. True
4. True
5. True

TEST YOUR KNOWLEDGE

PLANETARY HOURS

MIXED QUIZ

1. The planetary hour of war falls under what planet and day?
2. The planetary hour of love falls under what planet and day?
3. The Moon on Monday deals with the planetary hour of women's mysteries. (True or False)
4. Mercury on Wednesday deals with the planetary hour of thought processes and thinking. (True or False)
5. The planetary hour of prosperity and joy falls under what planet and day?

TEST YOUR KNOWLEDGE

ANSWER SHEET

1. Mars, Tuesday
2. Venus, Friday
3. True
4. True
5. Sun, Sunday

4

Elements and Their Use in Magick

To properly finish your magickal act, you must learn a little about the elements and how they are important to your work.

For the purposes of this book, we will consider the four basic elements: Earth, Fire, Air, and Water.

An element in metaphysics is considered to be one of the four basic components that make up life itself. These components all vibrate differently and to specific rhythms in life. When properly aligned with your goals, these elemental forces can help to produce the desired effect in your Candle Magick.

To properly complete your Candle Magick, you need to know which of the four elements best suits your needs and purposes. A reminder here: This is one of your dominoes, and must be carefully considered.

Each of the four elements has an energy and essence. By properly concluding your magickal act and giving to that essence what it likes best, you have honored it, and it will aid your desires. This could be wine for the Earth essence, sandalwood for the Fire essence, incense for the Air essence, and a crystal for the Water essence.

Each of these components has an associated geographical direction. The correct direction should be faced when dealing with each element. If you neglect this, it is like speaking to someone and turning your back to him or her. It is considered rude and can hinder your work.

TABLE 11

THE ELEMENTS

Earth:

Direction:	North/Material
Colors:	Browns, Blacks, (Whites) in some Native American systems, Purples, Greens
Elementals:	Gnomes
Season:	Winter
Ritual Symbol:	Pentacle
Favored Moon Phase:	Fourth Quarter
Favored Time:	Midnight
Key Words:	Patience, balance, death, strength, decay, health, stability
Feelings:	Dry and cold (dry ice)
To Complete:	Bury all magickal works facing the North.
Offerings:	Plants, incense, music, earth, foods, stones, wine, organic fertilizers.
Specific Offerings:	Honeysuckle, pine, musk, cedar, patchouly, jasmine.

Fire:

Direction:	South/Energy
Colors:	Reds, Oranges, Golds
Elementals:	Salamanders
Season:	Summer
Ritual Symbol:	Athame or Sword (Wands)
Favored Moon Phase:	Second Quarter
Favored Time:	Noon
Key Words:	Force, lust, fertility and virility, growth, rejuvenation, passion
Feelings:	Hot and dry (deserts)
To Complete:	Burn all magickal works;

	scatter or bury remnants to the South.
Offering:	Dried herbs or plants, incense, music, papers, dead woods.
Specific Offerings:	Carnation, rosemary, primrose, vanilla, cloves, cinnamon.

Air:

Direction:	East/Mental
Colors:	Blues, Yellows, Greens
Elementals:	Sylphs
Season:	Spring
Ritual Symbol:	Wand (Swords)
Favored Moon Phase:	First Quarter
Favored Time:	Dawn
Key Words:	Friendship, thought, memory, intellect, knowledge, persuasion, birth
Feelings:	Moist heat (tropical)
To Complete:	Scatter in the wind; burn or break into small pieces and face the East.
Offerings:	Dried herbs and plants, incense, music, soap bubbles, song, laughter, scattered bird seed.
Specific Offerings:	Spearmint, peppermint, eucalyptus, thyme, lavender, sandlewood.

Water:

Direction:	West/Emotion
Colors:	Blues, Whites, Light Grays, Pinks, Sea Greens
Elementals:	Undines
Season:	Fall
Ritual Symbol:	Cup/Chalice
Favored Moon Phase:	Full moon

Favored Time:	Dusk
Key Words:	Fertility, emotion, intuition, insight, womb, conception, pregnancy
Feelings:	Cold moisture (winter rains)
To Complete:	Throw into a body of water facing the West.
Offerings:	Flowers, water plants, incense, music, salt, breads, song, dance.
Specific Offerings:	Gardenia, geranium, rose, myrrh, violet, sweet orange.

There are colors that can be used for more than one element, depending on the element's base color. For example:

Earth/Browns, Blacks
Fire/Reds, Oranges
Air/Yellows, Sky Blues
Water/Blues, Sea Greens

These are generally accepted colors, and all others are secondary. Use your discretion as to whether you believe your Dark Gray candle should be used for the element of the North/Earth or West/Water, etc.

Begin to use your magickal intuition for solving such future questions—you will find it most reliable.

Disposing of Magickal Remnants

Ending your magickal work is one of the most important steps of all, so here are suggestions on how to properly dispose of any magickal remnants to your work—e.g., ashes, wax, incense.

Constructive Magick Only!

Earth/North
Bury your magick and give a crystal to help heal the Earth Mother.

Air/East

If possible and not polluting, scatter your magick to the winds. Or save remnants (usually only ash is left) and mix into the soil. Then plant a tree (or other vegetation) somewhere needed and add a crystal or charcoal. This helps to heal our atmosphere.

Fire/South

In your cauldron or barbecue pit (retained for magick only) burn your magickal remnants. Offer oils or resin incense to heal the war and strife in our world today. Once a sufficient amount has gathered, mix with a good plant compound and scatter in the garden, add crystal chips or charcoal.

Water/West

Grind up any remnants of your magick. Combine this with plant fertilizer and a good potting soil when watering your plants. If you have positively energized water, give them a drink (not your magickal bath water or salt water).

Destructive Magick

For destructive magick of all kinds, wrap up the contents into a biodegradable paper bag. Add one apple and small crystal. Add a good fertilizer and soil mix. Bury where you might want a tree to grow.

TEST YOUR KNOWLEDGE

THE ELEMENTS

MIXED QUIZ

1. Gnomes are found under what ruling element?
2. Sylphs are found under what ruling element?
3. Undines are found under what ruling element?
4. Salamanders are found under what ruling element?
5. Exercise: Use a candle that is dedicated to one of your four elements that you are especially drawn to. Ground, center, and prepare your Aura. Proceed to your special

place. Merge with the lit candle. Ask for a teacher. Then ask this master what you need to do to become his or her student. Record your findings in your Magickal Journal.

FOR YOUR NOTES

TEST YOUR KNOWLEDGE

ANSWER SHEET

1. Earth; North
2. Air; East
3. Water; West
4. Fire; South
5. Exercise—Self explanatory

PART SEVEN

The greatest revolution of our generation is the discovery that
human beings, by changing the inner attitudes of their minds,
can change the outer aspects of their lives.

—William James (1842–1910)

1

Putting It All Together

Now that you have developed a firm background on the various aspects that make up Candle Magick, you will find the
Tables of Associations quick and easy references. They are
summations, with brief highlights of the other chapters, and
will aid you in your creative endeavors.

By using the Magickal Worksheet and the various Tables in
conjunction, you will soon find yourself making complex magickal decisions.

By mixing and matching the various aspects involved in the
magickal process (refer to the Mixing and Matching Hours
Table), you will soon progress to advanced Candle Magick
with amazing speed and accuracy.

By using the Magickal Worksheet as your guide, and referring to the information provided within this book, you have
everything you need to create the simplest to the most complex Candle Magick.

Begin by reviewing the Simplified Mixed Table of Associations on page 175. The format is brief and easily understood. The table begins with days of the week and also provides a brief description of the individual trait of each day.

Next you will note that if you are using the Ruling Planet on its own day, the ruling hours will always be the first, eighth, fifteenth and twenty-second. This is a good rule of thumb to adhere to when performing simple Candle Magick. Unless you are performing Creative or Advanced Candle Magick, variance is not necessary.

The common or ideal color usage for the Planet and Day, along with the corresponding Element, is also provided in this table.

Once you have mastered the beginning portion of the workbook and are ready for more advanced techniques, the Advanced Table of Associations will prove invaluable. This advanced table provides additional information necessary to perform more precise and complicated Candle Magick. Again it is laid out in an easy, step-by-step style to ensure complete understanding. It begins where the Simplified Table left off.

Now review the Magickal Worksheet. This sheet is basically self explanatory and relatively uncomplicated. Be sure, however, that you do understand it before continuing on. It is the Magickal Worksheet section that brings together everything we have discussed. Any error here and you are likely to miss your target, the magickal goal. So take your time. Understand the theories and thoughts behind each section. Do not be afraid to go back and review any section you are unsure of. You will find that it is time well spent. The quicker you learn to think in magickal and creative terms, the easier you will find the logic of magick and the stronger the results will be.

2

The Worksheet Preparation Guide

Describe Goals/Desires: Condense your goals and desires into as few words as possible to minimize misinterpretation. Write them on the lines provided.

Desired Results: Write out how you envision your goals or desires being fulfilled. From what sources? Be specific.

Abbreviate the Above in Four Words or Less: Narrow down your desires to four key words that best describe what it is you want to accomplish with this magickal act. List them under this heading on your worksheet.

Colors: The references on pages 89–97 are for color. From them, choose the appropriate candle color for your work.

Fragrance: The fragrance tables on pages 102–105 will introduce you to the various oils and scents that can enhance your work.

Bath: Pages 107–109 guide you on the necessities of the ritual bath and its importance to your success in magick. Review this section carefully. If the magickal bath must be skipped for any reason, replace it with the cleansing of the Aura along with grounding and centering your energy.

Moon Phases: At this point, you must decide whether you are bringing something to you or are you pushing it away. If you are manifesting something, bringing something to you, check the waxing Moon line. If you want to dissolve something, push something away, check the waning Moon line. Refer to page 113.

Days of the Week: Review the table on pages 118–119. Note the days of the week and choose which of these would best fit what you want to do. Check that day on your sheet.

Planetary Hours: Review the table on pages 123–125. Note what hours best correspond with your desires. Mark the sheet accordingly.

Elements: Refer to the table on page 129. Here you will be introduced to the four elements and how to properly dispose of your work for the best results.

CHANT FOR OBTAINING YOUR GOAL OR DESIRE

State concisely what it is *you want to happen*. From this information, compose a short chant for your purpose.

CHANT OF HOW YOU SEE THE GOAL OR DESIRE MANIFESTED

Visualize the final result of your magickal act and *how it is to manifest for you*. Now compose a simple chant or rhyme to that effect. *Be sure* to include how or where you see your desires manifesting.

Magickal Journal: It is very important that you begin to keep a magickal journal. A journal helps you not only to repeat success, and to learn from your mistakes, but also to develop your own system of Candle Magick. As your magickal knowledge and your journal grow, you will be able to track your progress. As your abilities increase, so will your magickal experiences. These experiences are paths that can be followed over and over. You just have to remember how to get there and, trust us, you won't unless you write it down. Refer to page 182.

All the items listed on the worksheet are important to a successful magickal act. Please do not skip any of them. Give them your full attention. Note that chants, rhymes, and songs create an altered state of awareness. It is in this state that the subconscious most easily can be reached to obtain your desires. For the purpose of this workbook, repeat your chant, rhyme, or song at least three times unless otherwise designated.

CHECKOFF LIST

1. Review your worksheet for accuracy. If you are satisfied, proceed.
2. On the appropriate Moon phase, day and hour, find a secluded and quiet place to set up the items you have

determined essential to your magickal act.

3. Set up a table where it will be safe from animals, people and drafts.

4. Obtain a fireproof container about twelve inches high. Place four inches of sand or Johnny Cat in the bottom of the container. Also obtain a small sand- or Johnny Cat-filled bowl or some ready-made receptacle for incense. Not all pet litter sand is entirely fireproof, so use with caution.

5. Lay out your incense, oil, lighter, and candle on the table. Add pictures, hair, or any other items that will help you to concentrate on your goal.

6. Following the guidelines in the section on Magickal Bath, prepare and take your cleansing bath. If the Magickal Bath is not possible, at least clean your Aura and ground and center your energy.

7. If you are using a magickal circle, draw it at this time. Once your circle is in place, you may call in the quarters and any Deities that will be used. (See 13 below.)

8. Follow the guidelines under Dressing Your Candle. Energize it with whatever method you have chosen from the selections in this workbook. Refer to your worksheet for the chant you have created. Repeat the chant three times, unless the act calls for some other number of repetitions, while dressing your candle.

9. Light your candle. Let it burn down completely unless contra indicated by spell requirements.

10. Transform any remaining energy into a healing Pink or Green. Ground this energy into Mother Earth.

11. If you have called in the quarters and utilized Deities, thank them for their aid. Next, dismiss the Deities and then the quarters. Open your Magickal Circle at this time. (See 13 below.)

12. Follow the guidelines under Elements for finishing your magick. Your magickal act is now complete.

13. Special Note: Items 7 and 11 above are given here as a convenience to the reader. This workbook does not explain the requirements of Ritual Magick, i.e., circle construction, nor does it go into detail on the specific use of Deities and their energies. Ritual Magick is another

subject entirely. Candle Magick not only can be a part of Ritual Magick but can also stand by itself.

HOW LONG BEFORE I SEE RESULTS?

The answer here is based on several factors. A lot depends on the magnitude of the magickal act: How well you have aligned your dominoes? How well you have developed your abilities of Creative Visualization, Object Merging, and Energizing? How carefully you have selected the proper attributes from the tables? You can expect to see something happen for small projects within twenty-four hours. Very large projects could take several months to begin and several years to complete.

If you find that you are not getting the exact results desired in a timely manner, consider the following:

Have you followed the worksheet explicitly? Have you clearly stated what it is you want to occur and how it is to occur? How large a project are you undertaking? To influence something large, like winning a lottery, takes repeated effort. You must realize that there are many strong energies at work in the universe. Someone else maybe attempting to manipulate them as you are. Do not be discouraged though; magick has a way of building and becoming more powerful every time it is performed. Therefore, by repetition and perseverance, the weaker or beginning practitioner can achieve what the stronger or more experienced worker can.

Further, check your Aura and Chakras for energy blocks and debris. This can frequently hinder your work as nothing else can.

Finally, ask yourself if you have allowed yourself to become programmed for failure. Too often in our lives, we allow others to dictate who we are, what we are, and what we can and cannot expect to achieve in life. With magick, you dictate what you will or will not accept in your life. You must believe that what you are doing will work or you fail before you begin.

3

The Candle Magick Worksheet

WORKSHEET

DESCRIBE GOALS/DESIRES: _____ DATE: _____

_____

_____

_____

_____

DESIRED RESULTS: _____

_____

ABBREVIATE THE ABOVE IN FOUR WORDS OR LESS:

DESIRES: _____ / _____ / _____ / _____

COLORS: _____ _____

FRAGRANCE: _____ _____

BATH: _____

PREPARE MAGICKAL BATH: _____

CLEAN AURIC FIELD: _____

MOON PHASES
WAXING MOON: _____   WANING MOON: _____

DAY OF WEEK:
MONDAY: _____   TUESDAY: _____   WEDNESDAY: _____   THURSDAY: _____
FRIDAY: _____   SATURDAY: _____   SUNDAY: _____

PLANETARY HOURS:
_____ / _____ / _____

ELEMENTS: _____

CHANT FOR OBTAINING YOUR DESIRES/GOALS:

CHANT OF HOW YOU SEE THE GOAL OR DESIRE MANIFESTED:

SET UP TOOLS AND EQUIPMENT:

BEGIN YOUR MAGICK

YOUR NOTES:

4

Sample Candle Magick Worksheets

Candle Magick on a Waxing Moon

WORKSHEET

DATE: _9-1-91_

DESCRIBE GOALS/DESIRES: _Money_

I need more money in my life now.

DESIRED RESULTS:

I wish to be promoted at work and receive a pay raise.

ABBREVIATE THE ABOVE IN FOUR WORDS OR LESS:

DESIRES: _Promotion_ / _____ / _____ / _Pay raise_

COLORS:

Orange   _Yellow_   _Gold_

FRAGRANCE:

Rue   _Cloves_   _Rosemary_

BATH:

Herbs—None Now   _Rosemary Oils_   _Sea Salts_   _Color—Yellow_

PREPARE MAGICKAL BATH:

(For Your Notes)

CLEAN AURIC FIELD:

(For Your Notes)

MOON PHASES
WAXING MOON: _XXX_   WANING MOON:

DAY OF WEEK:
MONDAY: TUESDAY: WEDNESDAY: THURSDAY:
FRIDAY: SATURDAY: SUNDAY: _XXX_

PLANETARY HOURS:
_1st._ / _8th._ / _15th._ / _22nd._

ELEMENTS:
Fire

CHANT FOR OBTAINING YOUR DESIRES/GOALS:

Money like honey, stick to me

Promotion and pay raise

Manifest be . . .

CHANT OF HOW YOU SEE THE GOAL OR DESIRE MANIFESTED:

Accolades, praises for a job well done

Enhance the coffers of this Mother's son.

SET UP TOOLS AND EQUIPMENT:

(For Your Notes)

BEGIN YOUR MAGICK

YOUR NOTES:

WORKSHEET

DESCRIBE GOALS/DESIRES: *Protect My Health*　　　　DATE: *9-1-91*

I wish to protect and enhance my already robust good health.

DESIRED RESULTS:

Protection against failing health.

ABBREVIATE THE ABOVE IN FOUR WORDS OR LESS:

DESIRES: *Protection* / *Enhancement* / *of* / *Health*

COLORS:

Orange　　　　*Red*　　　　*Yellow*

FRAGRANCE:

Rue　　　　*Carnation*　　　　*Lilly of the Valley*

BATH:

Herbs-None Now   _Carnation Oils_   _Sea Salts_   _Color-Reds_

PREPARE MAGICKAL BATH: _____

_____ (For Your Notes) _____

_____

CLEAN AURIC FIELD: _____

_____ (For Your Notes) _____

MOON PHASES

WAXING MOON: ___ XXX ___   WANING MOON: _____

DAY OF WEEK:

MONDAY: ___ TUESDAY: _XXX_ WEDNESDAY: _XXX_ THURSDAY: _____

FRIDAY: ___ SATURDAY: ___ SUNDAY: _XXX_

PLANETARY HOURS:

_1st._ / ___ _8th._ / ___ _15th._ / ___ _22nd._

ELEMENTS: _____

Fire

CHANT FOR OBTAINING YOUR DESIRES/GOALS:

Robust I am,

Robust I'll Stay,

From very good health I will never stray

CHANT OF HOW YOU SEE THE GOAL OR DESIRE MANIFESTED:

Shield of health, protect me

Robust and hardy, I'll always be.

SET UP TOOLS AND EQUIPMENT:

(For Your Notes)

BEGIN YOUR MAGICK

YOUR NOTES:

WORKSHEET

DESCRIBE GOALS/DESIRES: _Protection_   DATE: _9-1-91_

To protect my family and myself from harm and negative influences.

_____

_____

_____

DESIRED RESULTS:

A cloak of protection around my family and myself.

_____

ABBREVIATE THE ABOVE IN FOUR WORDS OR LESS:

DESIRES: _Protection_ / _Against_ / _Negativity_ / _Harm_

COLORS:

Whites   _Pearls_

FRAGRANCE:

White Rose

BATH:

White Roses   _Rose Oils_   _Sea Salts_ _____

PREPARE MAGICKAL BATH:

(For Your Notes)

CLEAN AURIC FIELD:

(For Your Notes)

MOON PHASES

WAXING MOON: ___ XXX ___   WANING MOON: ___

DAY OF WEEK:

MONDAY: XXX   TUESDAY: ___   WEDNESDAY: ___   THURSDAY: ___

FRIDAY: ___ ***   SATURDAY: ___   SUNDAY: ___

PLANETARY HOURS:

1st. ___ / ___ 8th. ___ / ___ 15th. ___ / ___ 22nd. ___

ELEMENTS:

*(Earth)   Water   *(Air)

*Optional

CHANT FOR OBTAINING YOUR DESIRES/GOALS:

Family safe, family fine

No harm to us, from thee or thine

CHANT OF HOW YOU SEE THE GOAL OR DESIRE MANIFESTED:

A veil descends and shrouds us all

No enemy can come beyond that wall

SET UP TOOLS AND EQUIPMENT:

(For Your Notes)

BEGIN YOUR MAGICK

YOUR NOTES:

WORKSHEET

DATE: _9-1-91_

DESCRIBE GOALS/DESIRES: _Love_

I want to find the perfect mate for me.

_____

_____

_____

DESIRED RESULTS:

Happiness in a love relationship with my perfect mate.

_____

ABBREVIATE THE ABOVE IN FOUR WORDS OR LESS:

DESIRES: _Perfect_ / _Mate_ / _For_ / _Me_

COLORS:

_____ _Cherry-Red_ _____

FRAGRANCE:

Primrose _____ _Honeysuckle_ _____ _Thyme_

BATH:

Red Rose Petals   _Red Rose Oils_   _Sea Salts_   _Color—Reds_

PREPARE MAGICKAL BATH:

_____

_____ _(For Your Notes)_

CLEAN AURIC FIELD:

_____

_____ _(For Your Notes)_

MOON PHASES
WAXING MOON: _____ _XXX_ _____   WANING MOON: _____

DAY OF WEEK:
MONDAY: _***_   TUESDAY: _***_   WEDNESDAY: _____   THURSDAY: _____
FRIDAY: _XXX_   SATURDAY: _____   SUNDAY: _____

PLANETARY HOURS:
_1st._ / _____ _8th._ / _____ _15th._ / _____ _22nd._ / _____

ELEMENTS:
Air _____ _Water_ _____ *(Fire with Caution)

*Optional

CHANT FOR OBTAINING YOUR DESIRES/GOALS:

The perfect mate for me, I can clearly see.

Her heart sings out, as she hears my shout,

"I am the perfect mate for thee, come now, manifest for me."

CHANT OF HOW YOU SEE THE GOAL OR DESIRE MANIFESTED:

Her soul has heard my call, she stands beautiful, and tall.

With eyes of dancing light, she relieves my lonely plight.

With her love and laughter, I am happy, everafter.

SET UP TOOLS AND EQUIPMENT:

(For Your Notes)

BEGIN YOUR MAGICK

YOUR NOTES:

Candle Magick on a Waning Moon

WORKSHEET

DESCRIBE GOALS/DESIRES: _Stop Fear of Success_   DATE: _9-1-91_

I wish to eliminate the overriding fear of success.

_____

_____

_____

_____

DESIRED RESULTS:

To eliminate the mental block I have towards success.

_____

ABBREVIATE THE ABOVE IN FOUR WORDS OR LESS:

DESIRES: _Eliminate_ / _Fears_ / _Of_ / _Success_

COLORS:

*_(Yellows)_   _Purples_   *_(Oranges)_

FRAGRANCE:

Jasmine

_____

*Optional

BATH:
Jasmine Flowers _____ _Oils-Jasmine_ _____ _Sea Salt_ _____ _Colors—None_

PREPARE MAGICKAL BATH:
_____
_____ (For Your Notes)
_____

CLEAN AURIC FIELD:
_____
_____ (For Your Notes)

MOON PHASES
WAXING MOON: _____   WANING MOON: ____XXX____

DAY OF WEEK:
MONDAY: ___***___   TUESDAY: _____   WEDNESDAY: _____   THURSDAY: XXX
FRIDAY: _____   SATURDAY: ___***___   SUNDAY: _____

PLANETARY HOURS:
_1st._ __/__ _8th._ __/__ _15th._ __/__ _22nd._

ELEMENTS:
*_(Water)_ _____ _Air_ _____ *_(Earth)_

*Optional

CHANT FOR OBTAINING YOUR DESIRES/GOALS:

No obstacle to me, the fear of success

I'll cherish the moment, I've achieved my best.

CHANT OF HOW YOU SEE THE GOAL OR DESIRE MANIFESTED:

The block is gone, I fear no more

Only success is for me in store.

SET UP TOOLS AND EQUIPMENT:

(For Your Notes)

BEGIN YOUR MAGICK

YOUR NOTES:

WORKSHEET

DESCRIBE GOALS/DESIRES: _Eliminate Obstacles in Job_   DATE: _9-1-91_
I wish to eliminate all negativity preventing me from achieving my highest potential in my job

_____

_____

_____

DESIRED RESULTS:
The elimination of negative obstacles in my job that prevent my success in all I undertake.

_____

ABBREVIATE THE ABOVE IN FOUR WORDS OR LESS:
DESIRES: _Eliminate_   / _Obstacles_   / _Negativity_   / _(in my) Job_

COLORS:
    *(Gray)   Purples   *(Black)

FRAGRANCE:
                            Jasmine

*Optional

BATH:

Jasmine Flowers _____ _Oils-Jasmine_ _____ _Sea Salts_ _____ _Color-Purple_ _____

PREPARE MAGICKAL BATH: _____

(For Your Notes)

CLEAN AURIC FIELD: _____

_____

(For Your Notes)

MOON PHASES

WAXING MOON: _____ WANING MOON: _____ XXX

DAY OF WEEK:

MONDAY: _____ TUESDAY: _____ WEDNESDAY: _____ *** THURSDAY: _XXX_

FRIDAY: _____ SATURDAY: _____ SUNDAY: _____ ***

PLANETARY HOURS:

1st. ___ / ___ 8th. ___ / ___ 15th. ___ / ___ 22nd. ___

ELEMENTS:

*(Earth) _____ Air _____ *(Fire) _____

*Optional

CHANT FOR OBTAINING YOUR DESIRES/GOALS:

Negative vibes, be gone from me

A job success, I'll truly be.

CHANT OF HOW YOU SEE THE GOAL OR DESIRE MANIFESTED:

Adverse reaction to me be gone

Success for me comes with dawn.

SET UP TOOLS AND EQUIPMENT:

(For Your Notes)

BEGIN YOUR MAGICK

YOUR NOTES:

WORKSHEET

DESCRIBE GOALS/DESIRES: _Send Away Tired Feelings_   DATE: _9-1-91_

I wish to send away whatever is causing me to feel tired and rundown all the time.

_____

_____

_____

_____

DESIRED RESULTS:

I wish to feel energetic again.

_____

ABBREVIATE THE ABOVE IN FOUR WORDS OR LESS:

DESIRES: _Eliminate_ / _Tired_ / _Rundown_ / _Feelings_

COLORS:

*(Yellows)   _*(Oranges)_   _Greens_

FRAGRANCE:

Lilly of The Valley   _____

*Optional

BATH:

(optional) _____ _(optional)_ _____ _Sea Salts**_ _____ _Color—Green_ _____

PREPARE MAGICKAL BATH: _____

(For Your Notes)

_____

_____

CLEAN AURIC FIELD: _____

(For Your Notes)

_____

MOON PHASES

WAXING MOON: _____   WANING MOON: _____ XXX

DAY OF WEEK:

MONDAY: _____ TUESDAY: _____ WEDNESDAY: XXX THURSDAY: _____

FRIDAY: *** _____ SATURDAY: _____ SUNDAY: *** _____

PLANETARY HOURS:

1st. _____ / _____ 8th. _____ / _____ 15th. _____ / _____ 22nd. _____

ELEMENTS:

Earth _____   Air _____   Water _____

*Optional

CHANT FOR OBTAINING YOUR DESIRES/GOALS:

Tired and rundown no more be,

Return to health and vitality.

CHANT OF HOW YOU SEE THE GOAL OR DESIRE MANIFESTED:

Vaporous clouds ascend in league,

Taking with you all fatigue.

SET UP TOOLS AND EQUIPMENT:

(For Your Notes)

BEGIN YOUR MAGICK

YOUR NOTES:

WORKSHEET

DESCRIBE GOALS/DESIRES: _Unwanted Suitor Be Gone_   DATE: _9-1-91_

I wish to awaken an unwanted suitor to the fact I am not interested.

_____

_____

_____

_____

DESIRED RESULTS:

Awareness in my suitor that I am not available for a romantic relationship.

_____

ABBREVIATE THE ABOVE IN FOUR WORDS OR LESS:

DESIRES: _Awareness_ / _of_ / _Impossible_ / _Persuit_

COLORS:

Pearls   _Whites_   _Pastels_

FRAGRANCE:

White Rose

BATH:

Flower—Rose _Oil—Rose_ _Sea Salt_ _Color—Pink_

PREPARE MAGICKAL BATH:

_____

_____
(For Your Notes)

CLEAN AURIC FIELD:

_____

_____
(For Your Notes)

MOON PHASES

WAXING MOON:_____ WANING MOON:_____ XXX

DAY OF WEEK:

MONDAY: XXX TUESDAY:_____ WEDNESDAY:_____ THURSDAY:_____

FRIDAY:____ *** SATURDAY:____ *** SUNDAY:_____

PLANETARY HOURS:

1st. / 8th. / 15th. / 22nd.

ELEMENTS:

*(Air) Water *(Earth)

*Options

CHANT FOR OBTAINING YOUR DESIRES/GOALS:

Awaken suitor, hear my plea

My love for you, can never be.

CHANT OF HOW YOU SEE THE GOAL OR DESIRE MANIFESTED:

Reality comes to those who see

With me romance can never be.

SET UP TOOLS AND EQUIPMENT:

(For Your Notes)

BEGIN YOUR MAGICK

YOUR NOTES:

PART EIGHT

To read without reflecting is like eating without digesting.

—Edmund Burke (1729–1797)

1

Reference Tables at a Glance

MIXING AND MATCHING TABLE

COLOR	PEARLS	REDS	YELLOWS	PURPLES	GRNS/PINKS	BLACKS	ORANGES
WEEK DAYS	MONDAY	TUESDAY	WEDNESDAY	THURSDAY	FRIDAY	SATURDAY	SUNDAY
MEANINGS	EMOTION	ACTION	THOUGHT	EXPANSION	MANIFESTS	CYCLES	LIFE
MOON KEY WORD SPIRIT	WOMEN'S MYSTERIES GODDESS MAGICK	PATH OF THE AMAZON WARRIOR PREHISTORY	KNOWLEDGE OF ANCIENT MYSTERIES AND SECRETS	EXPANSION OF SPIRIT ASTRAL TRAVEL	THE GODDESS MANIFESTS WITHIN LOVE-SELF	THE CRONE DEATH'S DOOR ENDINGS BLOCKS	PERFECTION BALANCE YIN/YANG ETERNAL PATH
MARS KEY WORD AGGRESSION	ACTION AND AGGRESSION TEMPERED WITH FORESIGHT	PATH OF THE MALE WARRIOR CURRENT HISTORY	WISDOM IN WAR-GOVT, POLITICS COURTS LEADERSHIP	EXPANSION MILITARY INDUSTRY POLICE RELIGION	SEXUALITY LUST RAPE DESIRE POSSESSIVE	TO BLOCK- UNBLOCK PHYSICAL AGGRESSION AND DEATH	ATHLETICS GAMES HEALING VITALITY PROSPERITY
MERCURY KEY WORD WISDOM	LEARNING ANCIENT SECRETS LORE AND WISDOM	ACTION TEMPERED WITH GUILE OR WISDOM	SCHOLAR SCIENTIST HEALER SAGE EDUCATOR	GENIUS EGOMANIA INSANITY EXPLOSIVE- GROWTH	LOVING WITH WISDOM UNSELFISH LOVE	TO BLOCK- UNBLOCK MENTAL ILLNESS- PROBLEMS	HEALING THE MIND AND LEARNING TO HEAL
JUPITER KEY WORD GROWTH	EXPANDING SELF CHANNEL- SPIRITS & DIETIES	ANNIHILATE CONQUEST WORLD WAR DICTATOR TO WIN	INCREASE- LEARNING WISDOM SCHOOLS STUDENTS	RAPID- GROWTH AND EXPANSION UNCHECKED	GROWING LOVE INCREASE MATERIAL NEEDS	TO BLOCK- OR UNBLOCK EXPANSION & GROWTH	MONEY JOB PROMOTION SUPERIORS GOOD LUCK
VENUS KEY WORD LOVE	EARTH- MAGICK POWER- ANIMALS OLD-WAYS	SEX PASSION RAPE LUST SENSUALITY	WISDOM IN LOVE MENTAL ADORATION	CONSUMING -PASSION CREATING MORE HERE ON EARTH	PLEASURE DATING LOVERS ALL NEEDS FILLED	TO BLOCK- UNBLOCK MATERIAL NEEDS OR LOVE	PREGNANCY FERTILITY JOY NEW LIFE ABUNDANCE
SATURN KEY WORD DEATH	THE CRONE PAST LIVES OTHER WORLDS & DIMENSIONS	ILLNESS WAR DEATH ENDING BLOCKING	TO LEARN DEATH'S SECRETS KARMA THE VOID	TRANSMUTE GOVT. RELIGION INDUSTRY CULTURE	TO BLOCK- UNBLOCK RELATIONS FERTILITY NEEDS	TRANSMUTE OLD AGE CHANGE UNBLOCK BLOCK/END	ILLNESS IN PETS AND CHILDREN TO BLOCK- UNBLOCK
SUN KEY WORD BIRTH	PERFECT BALANCE HARMONY OF YIN/YANG	BIRTH OF AGGRESSION WAR ACTION OPPRESSION	KNOWLEDGE OF LIFE ON EARTH BIRTH OF WISDOM	REBIRTHING THE OLD KNOWLEDGE FOR THE NEW AGE	BIRTH-PETS & BABIES FERTILITY CHILDREN MOTHERS	TRANSMUTE PEOPLE ANIMALS PATH OR A PROJECT	MALE MYSTERIES THE GODS EXTERNAL PATH
STONES	MOON- STONES	BLOOD- STONES	TOPAZ	AMETHYST	TURQUOISE	ONYX	QUARTZ- CRYSTALS
CHAKRAS	SPLEEN	ROOT	SOLAR PLEXUS	CROWN	THROAT	THIRD EYE	HEART
METALS	SILVER	IRON	QUICK SILVER	TIN	COPPER	LEAD	GOLD
ELEMENTS	WATER	FIRE	AIR	EARTH-AIR ETHERIC FIRE	EARTH WATER	ETHERIC EARTH	FIRE AIR

MIXED TABLE OF ASSOCIATION

DAY	PLANET	ASSOCIATION	HOUR	COLOR	FRAGRANCE	ELEMENT
MON	MOON	WIVES, GIRLS, WOMEN'S MYSTERIES, HEALING, EMOTIONS, PROTECTION, GODDESS MAGICK AND GODDESSES	1 18 15 22	WHITES	MYRRH	WATER
TUES	MARS	COURAGE, WAR, ACTION, BATTLES, SPORTS, INDEPENDENCE, LUST, RAPE, STRENGTH, PHYSICAL ACTS	1 18 15 22	REDS	CARNATION	FIRE
WED	MERCURY	MENTAL, WISDOM, LEARNING, SCHOOLS, TEACHING, CLARITY, THOUGHT PROCESS, HEALING ARTS	1 18 15 22	YELLOWS	FERN	AIR
THURS	JUPITER	EXPANSION, POWER. FAME, WEALTH, SUPERVISORS, BUSINESS, OLDER PERSONS OF POWER	1 18 15 22	PURPLES	SAGE	EARTH AIR WATER FIRE ETHERIC
FRI	VENUS	LOVERS, LIFE, PETS. CHILDREN, PREGNANCY, BIRTH, FERTILITY, MATERIAL NEEDS. PLEASURE. AFFECTION	1 18 15 22	PINKS AND GREENS	ROSE	EARTH WATER
SAT	SATURN	BLOCKS. ENDINGS, TO STOP SOMETHING, DEATH, THE UNKNOWN. BREAKING OLD BONDS, CHAINS OR HABITS	1 18 15 22	BROWNS AND BLACKS	IRIS	ETHERIC EARTH
SUN	SUN	CHILDLIKE, INNOCENT, ADVENTURE. WEALTH, HUSBANDS, BOYS, GODS, NEW BEGINNINGS AND MALE MYSTERIES	1 18 15 22	ORANGES	CLOVES	FIRE AIR

TABLE OF DAY HOURS

WEEK DAYS / HOURS	MON	TUES	WED	THUR	FRI	SAT	SUN
1	☽ MOON	♂ MARS	☿ MERCURY	♃ JUPITER	♀ VENUS	♄ SATURN	☉ SUN
2	♄ SATURN	☉ SUN	☽ MOON	♂ MARS	☿ MERCURY	♃ JUPITER	♀ VENUS
3	♃ JUPITER	♀ VENUS	♄ SATURN	☉ SUN	☽ MOON	♂ MARS	☿ MERCURY
4	♂ MARS	☿ MERCURY	♃ JUPITER	♀ VENUS	♄ SATURN	☉ SUN	☽ MOON
5	☉ SUN	☽ MOON	♂ MARS	☿ MERCURY	♃ JUPITER	♀ VENUS	♄ SATURN
6	♀ VENUS	♄ SATURN	☉ SUN	☽ MOON	♂ MARS	☿ MERCURY	♃ JUPITER
7	☿ MERCURY	♃ JUPITER	♀ VENUS	♄ SATURN	☉ SUN	☽ MOON	♂ MARS
8	☽ MOON	♂ MARS	☿ MERCURY	♃ JUPITER	♀ VENUS	♄ SATURN	☉ SUN
9	♄ SATURN	☉ SUN	☽ MOON	♂ MARS	☿ MERCURY	♃ JUPITER	♀ VENUS
10	♃ JUPITER	♀ VENUS	♄ SATURN	☉ SUN	☽ MOON	♂ MARS	☿ MERCURY
11	♂ MARS	☿ MERCURY	♃ JUPITER	♀ VENUS	♄ SATURN	☉ SUN	☽ MOON
12	☉ SUN	☽ MOON	♂ MARS	☿ MERCURY	♃ JUPITER	♀ VENUS	♄ SATURN

DAYS OF THE WEEK DAYS	MONDAY	TUESDAY	WEDNESDAY	THURSDAY	FRIDAY	SATURDAY	SUNDAY
COLORS	WHITES	REDS	YELLOWS	PURPLES	PINKS	BLACKS	ORANGES
PLANET SYMBOLS	☽ moon	♂ mars	☿ mercury	♃ jupiter	♀ venus	♄ saturn	☉ sun
FRAGRANCE	GARDENIA MYRRH JASMINE	CARNATION PINE JASMINE	LAVENDER BAYBERRY TOBACCO	MAGNOLIA SAGE SANDLE WOOD	ROSE THYME LILAC	HYACINTH PATCHOULY VIOLETS	MARIGOLD CLOVES CINNAMON
HOURS OF MONDAY MOON	1,8,15,22	5,12,19	2,9,16,23	6,13,20	3,10,17,24	7,14,21	4,11,18
HOURS OF TUESDAY MARS	4,11,18	1,8,15,22	5,12,19	2,9,16,23	6,13,20	3,10,17,24	7,14,21
HOURS OF WEDNESDAY MERCURY	7,14,24	4,11,18	1,8,15,22	5,12,19	2,9,16,23	6,13,20	3,10,17,24
HOURS OF THURSDAY JUPITER	3,10,17,24	7,14,21	4,11,18	1,8,15,22	5,12,19	2,9,16,23	6,13,20
HOURS OF FRIDAY VENUS	6,13,20	3,10,17,24	7,14,21	4,11,18	1,8,15,22	5,12,19	2,9,16,23
HOURS OF SATURDAY SATURN	2,9,16,23	6,13,20	3,10,17,24	7,14,21	4,11,18	1,8,15,22	5,12,19
HOURS OF SUNDAY SUN	5,12,19	2,9,16,23	6,13,20	3,10,17,24	7,14,21	4,11,18	1,8,15,22

Magickal Journal

MAGICKAL JOURNAL

MAGICKAL JOURNAL

_____

_____

_____

_____

_____

_____

_____

_____

_____

_____

_____

_____

_____

_____

_____

_____

_____

_____

_____

Your Personal Journal

YOUR PERSONAL
JOURNAL:_____DATE_____

_____
_____
_____
_____
_____
_____
_____
_____
_____
_____
_____
_____
_____
_____
_____
_____
_____
_____
_____
_____
_____
_____
_____
_____
_____
_____

YOUR PERSONAL
JOURNAL:_____ DATE_____

_____

_____

_____

_____

_____

_____

_____

_____

_____

_____

_____

_____

_____

_____

_____

_____

_____

_____

_____

_____

_____

_____

_____

YOUR PERSONAL
JOURNAL:_____DATE_____

_____
_____
_____
_____
_____
_____
_____
_____
_____
_____
_____
_____
_____
_____
_____
_____
_____
_____
_____
_____
_____
_____
_____
_____
_____
_____

PART NINE

1

Exclusively Candles

By now, you should be familiar with the fundamentals of Candle Magick. Exclusively Candles takes this information a step further by giving you fresh insights into old and traditional lore, upon which we have based our unique system of Candle Magick. This will allow you to tailor your Candle Magick to your individual needs.

Some of you may have already browsed through the workbook and recognized the Devotional and Novelty candles used in Catholicism and what is commonly and erroneously lumped under the heading of Voodoo. There are several excellent books that deal with these topics individually. We will therefore mention them only where relevant.

Our own system of Candle Magick was developed over a period of thirty years. At the ripe old age of five, Kala was, as she called it then, "learning to be magickal," much to her mother's amusement. Her favorite pastime was candle crafting. Taking remnants of burnt candles, she melted them on a steam wall heater, which seemed to be in every home in Japan, and crafted people, animals, and talismans. Being raised among many nationalities and cultures in various nations gave her rare insight into the understanding of those cultures and an appreciation for their magick as well.

Kala's experience of being raised multinationally, combined with an intense interest in the properties of color and of Mother Earth, has led to our current system of magick which we call Earthcraft. We now share with you portions of it.

Earthcraft is a working combination of several systems, including some forms of Voodoo, as will be seen. H. V. Lampe has stated in his work *Famous Voodoo Rituals and Spells*, "As with a majority of religions, Voodoo varies in many details depending on locale and country."

So it will be with your magick as you develop your own working style and system. Once you teach it to another, it is no longer exclusively yours. It is forever changed. What worked for you may not work for another. Therefore, new practitioners will drop any portions of your Candle Magick that do not work for them, as you will add to and subtract from ours. Eventually, a whole new system, founded on old traditions, is created.

The freedom of Candle Magick to develop in this way is what has made it stand out from other systems of magick that wax and wane in popularity. By continually adopting new and improved methods, ideas, and even Deities, this system of magick remains ever popular and useful. The commonality found within the various methods of Candle Magick clearly shows the working roots of the system.

In her *Voodoo Handbook of Cult Secrets*, Anna Riva writes, "Voodoo ritual borrows heavily from Catholic services, including an altar covered with candles and surrounded by pictures of saints and along with the use of holy water...." Of course, the Catholic Church had previously borrowed magick and ritual knowledge from the predating pagans of Europe. So do not be shy. Adopt what works and throw out the rest. The real test of any magickal system is whether it works for you.

At all times, your magick must be teeming with emotion and energy to actually make it powerful. Contrary to some systems, we teach that the candle is to where all hate, envy, jealousy, greed, sorrow, and like emotions should go for proper transformation and constructive manifestation. Don't waste your anger or emotions on others. Put them into a candle and make that energy work for you, not against you by building up blocks in the Aura.

Think of your Candle Magick as a form of manifestation therapy. Use it to get rid of blocks and old hurts, and to better your life. That is exactly what it is meant for.

We have found that keeping one's Candle Magick as brief, simple, and to the point as possible, works far better than long complicated rituals. Too often, practitioners are concentrating on the next verse of a spell or act of physical obeisance rather than working on the necessary emotions and energies to do effective magick.

The key above all else, though, is to do what works best for you regardless of what others are doing or saying. So what if someone has many years of magickal experience and touts their method as the "only way." If it does not work for you, what good is it to you? If it works for you, then it's right for you. Narrow mindedness has no place in magick.

Charmaine Dey appropriately states in *The Magick Candle*, "There are no firm rules as to what must be said or done in each case, in order to effect a successful candle spell. . . . Some may achieve results by burning a single candle with a purpose firmly in mind. Others may do better with an elaborate ceremony. . . ." We totally agree.

Sympathetic Magick

Sympathetic Magick often makes use of various items such as pictures, personal effects, personal data (driver's license numbers, phone numbers, addresses, employee numbers, Social Security numbers), and parts of the body such as fingernail clippings and hair. Anything that is considered unique to the individual or animal may be used.

These unique items are used in several different ways to enhance your magick. They are used to personalize the candle.

Photographs, drivers' licenses, or marriage certificates are generally placed in front of or around the candle and should be protected from the wax and flame.

Personal body items should be blended into the wax when making the candle (destructive magick) or attached so that they will not burn as the candle burns (constructive magick).

Information such as names, numbers, and birth dates

should be inscribed directly into the candle. Some, however, prefer to write the information on parchment and attach it to the bottom of the candle. Either way will suffice.

These methods of personalizing a candle usually work best on, but are not limited to, an Image Candle. When you inscribe personal information and place a photograph of the person or animal on the altar, you have a very potent combination for influencing others in situations requiring enhancement of love, health, employment, protection, and life. Obviously, the reverse is also true.

By adding the personal body parts onto or into the candle, i.e., hair to head, picture to face, and naming the candle after the persona or animal, you thus create what is called a poppet of wax. This combination of all items can be dangerous to the novice magickian as well as the subject personified. You should not use this poppet for minor love, job, money, or similar spells. You can achieve a life or death control here resulting in tremendous karma. This poppet is a last resort item to preserve your own or another's life from a rapist, child molester, or murderer, or even from disease.

What is actually happening is that the minature (candle) becomes a representation of the original whole (person or animal) right down to the energy patterns. Some magickians equate this to a hologram where any small fraction of the whole has all the characteristics and energy patterns of the complete model. Thus anything done to the miniature replica will happen to the original.

Dr. June Bletzer defines Sympathetic Magick, in her *Encyclopedia Psychic Dictionary*, this way: ''to stimulate a likeness of, or to imitate a condition, object, or event in smaller form to cause a parallel in the condition, object or event; the action of things on one another through a secret affinity which is caused by some likeness in outward structure or reciprocal condition. . . .''

She further states: ''Holograh-oneness of all things; a unified, interrelated living whole unit having no beginning or ending, constantly printing its likeness in all sizes, shapes, and forms of living material; everything is a small piece of the whole, containing the same information and life, only reduced in size, shape, texture, speed, etc.''

In other words, we represent a higher order or whole while each of our cells represents us in miniature. Anything done to one of these cells will be registered on the whole.

Thought Form Creation

Thought form creation employs one or more of the methods of energy usage to create what we call a "Living Candle." In other words, the candle takes on a life and purpose of its own in accordance with the will and programming techniques of the practitioner. This creation of a "life" is a highly specialized form of candle energizing that requires you to use extreme care and should not be indulged in until you master the basic techniques. Be very careful not to deviate from what we outline until you have developed a thorough understanding of exactly what you are doing.

The purpose of a Living Candle is to create a thought form, housed within the wax, that will serve a single function and purpose for as long as the candle burns. The Living Candle embodies a portion of your personal Life Force, along with your emotions and will, for goal manifestation. The common candle embodies only your energy and will. Once the Living Candle burns out, all you have imbued within it fades out. The energy is reabsorbed into the source from which it was taken. In this case, you are that source.

Using outside energy to create the Living Candle requires more caution than just using your own energy. Outside energy is harder to control. The creation tends to act more like a familiar than a Living Candle. However, if you follow our methods as outlined, you should have no trouble.

As previously stated in this workbook, keeping your dominoes in line is essential to achieving the proper result from your magickal act. It is especially important here to keep proper notes and to outline your intentions in advance by using either the worksheet or your magickal journal. This is valuable information that you will need in case your magick goes awry and you have to repeat it or possibly even undo it. Always keep your magickal notes in a safe storage place.

Creating the Living Candle

Choose your energy source from one of the methods outlined in the workbook (Techniques of Candle Energizing). We recommend using the basic or personal energy if this is your first time attempting this advanced technique as the other energy sources can become quite independent, as previously mentioned.

Create a chant that outlines your purpose and will as you did in basic Candle Magick. Always state a single, clear purpose. A thought form cannot understand garbled instructions or multiple tasks. It cannot differentiate between right and wrong. If you do not understand the exact end result you are manifesting and cannot articulate it clearly, the thought form will be confused and the results unpredictable.

Always, always, always, remember to give your Living Candle the instructions for its time of termination. Do not get lazy and allow the thought form to live longer then designated. Even the most advanced practitioners of magick have a healthy respect for thought forms and their use. Once a thought form is out of control, it can act similar to a poltergeist. So always give the entity a definite birth and termination point. This instruction will usually be included in your chant, rhyme, or song.

The FIRST time you vocalize your chant is when you are anointing the candle and imbuing it with your energy and will.

The SECOND time is while you are lighting the candle, again imbuing it with your will and energy.

The THIRD time is just after you have lit the candle. Concentrate very intently upon your purpose and will until you feel that your candle fully understands its purpose.

An example of a chant you might try adapting to your own needs is as follows:

I GIVE YOU LIFE. I GIVE YOU POWER.
TO SERVE MY PURPOSE. TO SERVE MY WILL
AS YOUR FLAME GROWS STRONGER, SO WILL YOUR DESIRE
TO SERVE MY PURPOSE, TO SERVE MY WILL.
I GIVE YOU LIFE THIS DAY OF _____.
I GIVE YOU LIFE THIS HOUR OF _____.

TO SERVE MY PURPOSE. TO SERVE MY WILL.
AS YOUR FLAME BURNS ON, YOUR LIFE WILL FLOW.
AS YOUR FLAME DIES OUT, YOUR LIFE WILL GO.
YOU'LL CEASE TO BE AN ENTITY,
THUS HAVING FULFILLED YOUR DESTINY.
MY WILL AND DESIRES ARE [YOUR OWN RHYME]
I LIGHT YOUR WICK AND GIVE YOU LIFE.

Referring back to the Candle Magick Worksheet will be invaluable here for assistance in clarifying your will and exactly how you want to achieve your goal.

The advantages to using the Living Candle method of Candle Magick are many. It is valuable when a persistent form of magick is needed. You can imbue life into a twelve-day candle and use it to support other forms of magick. This is one of the best forms of magick to use when fighting illness. The thought form can be created to feed on the disease.

Candles for Advanced Magick

Adam and Eve Candles: These are human figure candles that come in a variety of colors. They can be used for anything from love (Pink) to gaining a new job (Green). Just use your imagination and the charts and tables in this workbook.

Altar Candles: The Altar Candles are used to represent the Deities or Powers with which you wish to communicate. This is a method of honoring them and their presence while tapping into their energy.

Two Altar Candles are placed on the altar, one to the left side and one to the right. The candles must always be taller and longer burning than any others on the altar. They must be lit first and extinguished last. Which of the Altar Candles is lit first depends upon the type of magick you are performing.

Color notwithstanding, the right candle represents male energy while the left represents female energy. Colors representing these male and female aspects of the same force will vary from system to system and from Deity to Deity.

Astral Candles: These are ''Personal Candles'' of colors and shapes that *feel* right for you or another person. They are not to be confused with Zodiac Candles (listed later) that are affixed to you by birth sign.

Astrological Candles: See Zodiac Candles.

Cat Candle: The Cat Candles are used for luck, jinx-breaking, and hexing, depending on the oils and energies placed into the candle. They usually are found in three basic colors:

• Black: used to banish bad luck and bring good luck. Gamblers should alter burning times between seven and eleven minutes per night.

• Red: generally used for gaining the love of another by feminine (feline) guile.

• Green: can be used to obtain money of a transient nature or to heal a sick pet.

Compass Candle: A Compass or Directional Candle is employed to help you determine a specific direction to take in life. It is usually a taper that drips freely when lit.

After assigning each of the four quarters a direction that you believe you would like your life to proceed in, observe the burning candle closely. The wax will drip in the direction that is best for you to take, not necessarily the one you might want, but you will be told what is best based on your present abilities.

Cross or Crucifix Candle: Sometimes referred to as the "Flora" or "Floral Cross" Candle, this comes in a variety of colors. It is generally burnt for protection and banishing. It can be used to represent angels which are called in to protect the home. One angel for each day of the week in the appropriate color.

Dehexing Candle: The best colors of Dehexing Candles are Gray, Silver, Black, or bi-colored Reversible Candles.

• Black: absorbs anything coming to you.

• Gray: neutralizes anything coming to you.

• Silver: reflects the incoming energy back to the sender. The curse, jinx, or crossing that was meant for you now rests on the sender. With the gray color, your energy must remain neutral.

• Reversible Color: is usually found in a combination of Red and Black, with the Black absorbing the incoming energy and the Red concentrating it, adding any tidbits of your making, and returning it to the sender with interest.

Devil Candle: This ominous candle is used to banish a jinxed or crossed condition in the home or place of employment, or about one's person. It is commonly used to exorcise someone of undesirable habits, energies, and entities. Mainly used in conjunction with the Psalms. It can also be used to create a jinx, hex, or crossed condition.

Devotional Candle: Devotional Candles, a form of Novena Candle, are usually those found in picturesque, heat resistant glass containers. The pictures on the glass are usually of various Saints or Loas while a prayer is normally inscribed on the reverse.

Double/Triple Action Candle: Double Action Candles have two colors. They are usually referred to as dual action or dual purpose candles. Exemplified by the Red and Black Reversible Candle mentioned above.

Triple Action Candles have one more color than the double action ones, hence one more action in combination. As an example, a typical triple action combination would be Red (passion), White (protection), and Green (money).

Floating Wick Candle: This candle merely exchanges the wax body for one of fragrant oils. A floating wick is suspended in the oil that lies within a decorative holder. These not only are beautiful for social gatherings, but can remove stale cooking or smoke odors as well. You also can energize the oil body as you would a wax body, but you must do so through the glass container as the oil has no solid structure.

Glass Oil Candle: Though similar to the Floating Wick Candle by virtue of using oil instead of wax in a (glass) container, the Glass Oil Candle's wick does not float. It is suspended into the oil body from a separate metal or glass fixture. The Glass Oil Candle comes in a variety of shapes, sizes, and colors, and is extremely useful in magick as a Perpetual Flame or Altar Candle. The fragrant oils can be changed to match the magick you are performing. The thick glass is usually safe and heat resistant.

The container usually has a small opening where new oil can be added without extinguishing the flame. As many of the containers are transparent, it is easy to see when the oil needs replacing.

As an Altar Candle for a magickal act, use the glass tapers. A neutral yet high vibrational oil in a thick crystal taper burns long after your magick is complete.

When using the Glass Oil Candle in a magickal act, always imbue the container first with your will. Do not anoint the container, however. Instead, with your will, imbue the oil meant to go into the container. In this way, the container has stored energy and power along with the oil.

Hand of Glory Candle: The Hand of Glory Candle and spell dates well into the early Middle Ages. According to Anna Riva in *Candle Burning Magick*, the spell was attributed to Albertus Magnus. Whether Magnus was the originator of this work or was simply passing on even older folk lore is not known.

The real danger of not understanding the "whys" or "hows" of magick is well depicted with this legend. *It also illustrates the real need for you to master the basics and then build upon them for your own true understanding of magick.*

There are several legends on how to obtain and use the Hand of Glory. Generally, the hand of a hanged thief or some successful criminal (at least until he was hanged) was taken, then processed and dipped into hot wax. The hand was then set afire so that the light from it would render its carrier invisible, along with paralyzing anyone seeing it.

Before you start digging around in your local graveyard, let's examine the thoughts behind this magickal legend.

First, the taking of the hand of an executed man, once a thief, now a spirit and invisible to mortal eyes, was believed to bestow this invisibility trait on the possessor.

Second, the legend is so incomplete that the exact "facts" cannot be ascertained. You can do much better with Creative Visualization or Candle Magick and leave the hands with the owners.

With Creative Visualization, you can cloak yourself in a cloud of mist using the energy from the solar plexus. This raises the bodily vibrations to the point of invisibility. Ketz uses this method on our car when a traffic cop is getting ready to pounce. Remember though to lift the veil before driving off or you may find yourself in frequent auto accidents!

With Candle Magick, you can control the mind of those you wish to be invisible to by using image candles. By willing others not to see you, you can come and go as you please.

Combining the two methods for a more theatrical approach, obtain some graveyard dust. Create a white, wax, image candle of yourself. Conjure your magick around your will and desire to become invisible to others. As you burn the candle, envision yourself surrounded by a white cottony substance. This takes a lot of concentration, since anytime you lose your concentration, you drop the veil and again will be visible.

The Guardian Flame Candle: There are many magickians who will only light a ritual candle with the "Sacred Flame" that has been dedicated to a Deity. This flame stands as a guardian in the home or temple. The Glass Oil Candle is excellent for this purpose.

Household Candle: An all-purpose candle used for magick.

Invocation Candle: An Altar Candle used to invoke a specific Deity. The Seven-Day Novena Candle is frequently used as an Invocation Candle as it is tall and will normally outlast other candles on the altar.

Jumbo Candle: A larger, thicker version of the Household Candle.

Knob Candle: This candle has seven small knobs, one atop another, and stands approximately seven inches high. One knob can be burnt each day while concentrating on what you desire to manifest into your life. A separate oil is used for each knob or an all purpose oil can be used on all seven knobs, the choice is yours.

The Black Seven Knob Candle provides an excellent way to banish undesirable energies from your home and the surrounding area. Burn one knob each day, starting on the Full Moon and working until the New Moon for best results. Use a Green Seven Knob Candle or a White Seven Day Candle to build a protective wall around your home and those you love.

Mummy Candle: Traditionally, this candle is used to acquire success and power. We prefer to use it to ward off illness, dangerous situations, or the specter of death.

Novelty Candle: Any candle that is not housed in glass and has a shape other than cylindrical. Some examples of the Novelty Candle are the Cat Candle, the Skull Candle, the Seven Knob Candle, and the Adam and Even Candles.

Novena Candle: Generally, this is a seven- to twelve-day, glass-enclosed candle. Frequently it is inscribed with pictures of various Saints along with prayers or chants on the reverse.

Seven-Day Novena: This long burning candle is housed

within a thick, heat resistant glass, and comes in three varieties: the Plain Novena, the Spiritual Novena, and the Specialty Novena. Each comes unscented and in a variety of colored wax and glass casings.

Plain Novena: This is an unmarked Seven-Day Candle found in a variety of colors.

Spiritual Novena: This candle comes with various depictions of Saints or Holy Personages on the glass container along with specific prayers or petitions to that Saint. The scene in which the Saint is depicted is usually a clue as to the Saint's power and use.

Specialty Novena: This candle is made of specific colors and sports specific designs on the glass container. It is named for the various actions it is to perform, and is often confused with the Novelty Candle. Remember, Novelty Candles do not come in glass containers and are not cylindrically shaped. Their names include Lucky 13, Controlling, Double Action, Reversible, and many others.

Offertory Candle: This is the name for the main candle that offers your desires, goals, or wishes out to the Universe for manifestation. It is also known as a Purpose Candle.

Phallus Candle: A candle in the shape of the male organ, it can be used for anything dealing with male sexuality, sterility, or impotence.

Protection Candle: A candle of any shape or size. The color here is what counts. Burn a White candle or a Saint Candle whenever doing destructive magick (banishing disease, for example) to protect yourself from harm. Also use Silver if you are doing destructive magick against another person who also knows magick.

Should your magick return unexpectedly, neutralize it with a Gray candle.

Some Novena Candles are considered Protection Candles. San Capistrano to keep away enemies; Saint Anthony for a job; Saint Jude for court problems; Sacred Heart for Marriage; Saint Clara for drug and addiction problems; Saint Michael for general protection. Whenever using the Saints, always write down your desire nine times on parchment and tape it to the candle bottom.

Using the Saints is not hard as the prayers are usually

inscribed right onto the candle containers.

Rebirthing Candle: A candle, with three or more days of burning time, that is used to guide the dead across to peace and rest.

Skull Candle: This candle, shaped in the form of a human skull, comes in several colors, the most common of which are Black, White, Red, and Green.

Traditionally, the Green Skull is used to make someone who is gullible easier to separate from his or her money. It can also be used to heal a mental or physical disorder of the mind, brain, or cranium. We have used the Green Skull to aid in memory retention for college.

A Friend of Kala's had a brain tumor and asked for help. As the Black Skull is normally used to cause great harm, suffering and pain, Kala focused that destructive power and directed it toward the tumor. It stopped enlarging and could then be safely removed by surgery. She then used the Green Skull on a waxing Moon to promote health and healing.

The Red Skull could be used to force someone physically to move away or to make him or her fall out of love with another person. Of course, the reverse could also be attempted depending on the Moon cycle.

The White Skull Candle can also be used for healing. In some traditions, after the proper healing oils are anointed into the candle, the 23rd Psalm is read over the sick or dying individual.

The White Skull Candle is the best one to use to bend someone to your will, contrary to our chart, as the Yellow Skull is very hard to find. This is a very good reason to learn to make your own candles.

Skull Candles of the appropriate colors can be of great aid to activists who must deal with bureaucracies. The large entities can be equated to headless monsters that feed off the life energies of their employees. By using the Skull Candle to represent the thought form of the bureaucracy, you can tap this thought form's energy and thus control much of what happens to it. By making the thought form feed upon itself, you can destroy it or allow it to restructure.

Snake or Bust Away Candle: This is a candle used to break free or "bust away" from evil. We use it to break free of undesirable conditions, situations, and habits.

Specialty Candle: The same as the Speciality Novena Candle mentioned previously. As the use of Novena and Speciality Candle varies a bit from our own method of Candle Magick, the colors, oils, and traditional meanings will vary slightly from what has been taught in this workbook. As Anna Riva has a wonderful book entitled *Devotions to the Saints*, further reference is not required here.

Vigil Candle: Any candle will suffice when burnt not only for a long period of time for another's benefit but also to peacefully demonstrate for a cause or action.

Witch Candle: Traditionally used as an extremely potent love candle, the idea being to ''bewitch'' your intended.

Yoni Candle: The female counterpart of the Phallus Candle. Shaped like a vulva, this candle is used in sex magick, safe birthing, and most anything dealing with women and their sexuality.

Zodiac or Astrological Candle: This candle is used to represent each of the twelve zodiacal signs. It is specifically colored, scented, and adorned with the information pertinent to the individual sign. Its use, normally in conjunction with other candles, is to represent the practitioner or another person in Candle Magick. As an example, one candle on an altar could represent your goal or target. The Zodiac Candle would be placed on the altar and then moved closer to the target candle to simulate the merging of the two.

On the next few pages, we have listed the twelve zodiacal signs and their related colors, planets, and most powerful weekdays.

Zodiac Candles

ARIES

March 20th to April 20th
Most powerful day of the week—Tuesday
Ruling Planet—Mars
Color Red

TAURUS

April 21st to May 20th
Most powerful day of the week—Friday
Ruling Planet—Venus
Color Pink

GEMINI

May 21st to June 24th
Most powerful day of the week—Wednesday
Ruling Planet—Mercury
Color Yellow—Green

CANCER

June 25th to July 23rd
Most powerful day of the week—Monday
Ruling Planet—Moon
Color White

LEO

July 24th to August 22nd
Most powerful day of the week—Sunday
Ruling Planet—Sun
Color Orange

VIRGO

August 23rd to September 22nd
Most powerful day of the week—Wednesday
Ruling Planet—Mercury
Color Yellow

LIBRA

September 23rd to October 22nd
Most powerful day of the week—Friday
Ruling Planet—Venus
Color Light Brown

SCORPIO

October 23rd to November 22nd
Most powerful day of the week—Tuesday
Ruling Planet—Mars
Color Red

SAGITTARIUS

November 23rd to December 22nd
Most powerful day of the week—Thursday
Ruling Planet—Jupiter
Color Purple

CAPRICORN

December 23rd to January 20th
Most powerful day of the week—Saturday
Ruling Planet—Saturn
Color Black

AQUARIUS

January 21st to February 20th
Most powerful day of the week—Saturday
Ruling Planet—Saturday
Color Dark Blue

PISCES

February 21st to March 19th
Most powerful day of the week—Thursday
Ruling Planet—Jupiter
Color Bright Royal Blue

TEST YOUR KNOWLEDGE
EXCLUSIVE CANDLES
TRUE OR FALSE

1. There is only one way to perform Candle Magick.
2. Candle Magick can be used as therapy.
3. Short uncomplicated Candle Magick generally works better than long complicated rituals.
4. The key to successful Candle Magick is to do what works best for you.
5. Personal items from another can be used to create a miniature of that person.
6. A Thought Form can be defined as molding energy into a living entity to serve a specific purpose and function for the creator.
7. Thought Forms are useful creatures that, once created, can be used over and over for complex tasks.
8. It is important to give any Thought Form a date or birth and a date of death.
9. The Devil Candle is used to conjure and worship the devil.
10. The Black Seven Knob Candle is used to banish undesirable energies.
11. Any candle that represents your desire or will to obtain something is called a Purpose or Offertory Candle.
12. A Skull Candle is excellent for representing large bureaucracies.
13. A Black Skull Candle can be used to banish disease.
14. Altar Candles can be Seven- or Twelve-Day Novena Candles.
15. Glass candles filled with oil can be energised for magickal use.

FOR YOUR NOTES

TEST YOUR KNOWLEDGE

ANSWER SHEET

1. False—The ways to perform Candle Magick are limited only by your imagination.
2. True
3. True
4. True
5. True
6. True
7. False—A Thought Form has the mentality of a three- to five-year-old at best. However, unlike the five-year-old, the Thought Form does not understand compassion, right, wrong, or love. This makes them potentially dangerous so should be terminated at the end of the magickal art.
8. True
9. False—It is used to banish a jinxed condition.
10. True
11. True
12. True
13. True
14. True
15. True

2

Techniques of Candle Energizing

Basic Energizing: There are many and varied basic methods of energizing a candle. Almost as many basic techniques exist as there are people energizing. The one common factor in all the basic techniques, though, is that the candle is imbued with the energy of the practitioner only. No outside energies are employed. This type of energizing is of the simplest type and the easiest to do.

Most users of these basic techniques are the chanters, the demonstrators, the dancers, and most practitioners of *basic* Candle Magick. They vary their methods by employing prayers, chants, dances, songs, meditation, or any combination of techniques that work for them. The large religious or vigilance gathering that utilizes the massed personal energy of many individuals is an example of this basic technique.

As a solo practitioner, you can also use this basic methodology. You must remember, though, that this methodology relies solely on your energy. Enough energy must be generated from within you to appropriately manifest your desired goal. This requires you to be strong both mentally and physically.

The candle will draw energy from you as it burns since you are its original energy source. Sometimes, depending on the magnitude of the magickal act, this can create a tired and listless feeling. To avoid this, make sure that you have supplied the candle with sufficient energy initially to perform the act. Even then, circumstances may require additional energy from

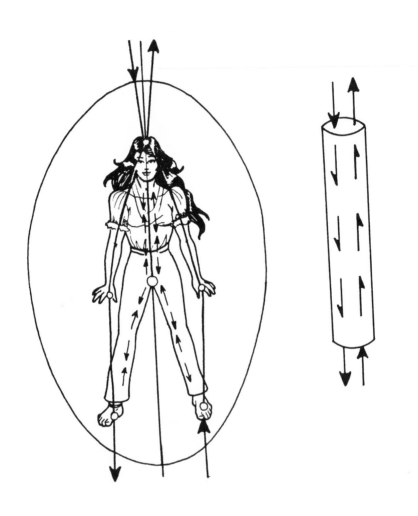

you or your candle can fail due to a lack of the needed magickal energy.

If you are quite sure your candle has enough energy to perform its task, detach yourself from it by severing all astral cords attached to your solar plexus. Then, put the magickal act out of your mind. Otherwise, your thoughts, worries, and concerns about the manifestation of your magick will drain both you and your candle.

Another point to remember here is that when you complete your energizing phase, be sure to ground the excess energy back to Mother Earth. By transmuting any stray or excess energy to a Pink or Green color and returning that energy via your grounding cord, obnoxious and mischievous entities cannot feed upon it. The returning of the energy also enhances the health of Mother Earth.

Finally, the basic method of energizing a candle solely with your own energy is a convenient method for quick and simple Candle Magick.

Using Earth Energy: Unlike the basic method where all energy comes from you, the utilization of earth energy adds an additional source for you to tap when performing magick. The tapping of the surrounding earth energy is often referred to as Earth Magick.

There are two common ways to tap into the source. The first you perform by creatively visualizing the drawing of energy up from the earth, passing it through your body, and then pushing it out into the candle. Here you expend less of your own energy and also give the candle a convenient source of additional energy if needed.

The theory behind using the energies of the Earth Mother is that manifestation is much easier due to the ample energy supply. And, since She is our Mother, the use of Her energy not only balances the elements in our bodies, but helps to balance our lives as well.

The second method encompasses the use of a magickal circle. This use of the circle is an effective way to retain in place all energy, created by Tantra (sex magick), singing, and chanting, until that energy can be effectively used.

Working within the magickal circle is recommended for anyone with weak creative visualization skills and low self energy. This makes it a good stepping stone for the beginner when progressing from basic to advanced magick.

The drawbacks to using a circle of energy from Mother Earth are that you must have ample space for a three-, six-, nine-, or twelve-foot diameter circle, depending on altar size and the number of magickal participants. You also must allot more time to the preparation of the act. The optional aspect of invoking, calling, and requesting the quarters will discourage an impatient practitioner. Circle Magick is better suited to Ritual and other types of magick rather than basic Candle Magick. If you wish to pursue this, there are many excellent books on Wiccan Ritual Magick available. (Refer to Suggested Readings.)

Using Universal Energy: Many practitioners complain that the universal energies are too severe, cold, impartial, and unpredictable for their needs. This is why many will use only the energy of the Earth Mother.

We have found this to be true, but to a limited degree. Humans and the Earth make up, after all, but one tiny cell in a much larger organism of life. Whatever the consensus, the Universe is a powerful source of energy. It is just more complicated and more difficult to control for some people. Utilizing its energy requires a more highly developed knowledge and skill foundation.

We have tapped into a translucent, almost irridescent plasma that can be drawn from the Universal source of energy that is warm, personal, and very obliging. The small sparks of color within this plasma are actually alive and offer healing and other energies to all who need them.

We also draw upon a feminine energy plasma of pearlesque white. It is extremely helpful in Kala's Feminine Spirituality activities. It is easy to channel and will not short circuit the Chakras or the auric field.

The universal energies are brought into the body by way of the Crown Chakra. It is then circulated throughout the body, brought into the hands, and then imbued into the candle. This process is similar to that when utilizing Earth energy except you use the Crown Chakra for entry and the Chakra energy runs in reverse of the Earth energy. However, excess energy is returned not to the Universe, but to Mother Earth by grounding it. The way we treat Her, She needs all the help She can get.

By tapping into the universal energy source, you have access to an unlimited supply of power and energy. It is easily drawn into your body and projected into the object. A magickal circle is not required due to the abundance of energy. You may use the circle if the energy must be channeled very precisely to its destination.

A word of caution is necessary here regarding the use of universal energy. The color, brilliance, and power of the energy must be carefully regulated when brought into your body. An energy too intense or too powerful can cause problems with the auric field and Chakras. It can also affect your ability to stay grounded and centered within the Aura itself. You can equate this to your plugging a 110-volt appliance into a 220-volt socket. Crash and burn.

Using the Life Force Energies: Life Force Energies is another term for using both the potent energy of the Universe and the more intimate energy of Mother Earth. A well-balanced combination of both these energies, coupled with your own internal energy, provides the ideal setting for your most powerful healing and strongest manifestations. There is no need for a long, elaborate ritual, magickal circle, or altar when using the Life Force Energies. A simple candle, the power of Creative Visualization, a strong desire, and emotion are all you need. This method offers a perfect balance of energy from above, below, and within for the attainment of successful Candle Magick. There is no need to worry about short circuiting if you follow our methods as described in this workbook.

They also help to heal the human body, balance the Chakras and auric field, and to keep you grounded, centered within the Aura, and in touch with the higher elements of power. We believe this method to be an ideal, all purpose method for generic Candle Magick.

The Use of Foreign Energies: Foreign energies are usually thought of as Gods, Goddesses, Angels, Loas, Saints, and sometimes pure elementals. The Deities are frequently pure beings of vibrating energy that have specific functions and attributions. Their energy can be utilized by you in what is referred to as Speciality Candle Magick. Their specific candles are called Devotional, Novena, Spiritual, and Novelty Candles.

The Spiritual Novenas usually are made to resemble the specific Deity in shape or have imprints on the cylindrical glass candles. Often prayers, meditations, chants, or invocations can be found inscribed somewhere on or in the candle.

Further, the shape of the candle may be of significance. Some Deities are frequently associated with specific shapes of candles such as Bast, the Cat Candle; Saturn, the Skull Candle; Satan, the Devil Candle; Saint Patrick, the Snake Candle; and Angels, the Cross or Floral Candle.

There are several ways of tapping into the energy of a Deity for your Candle Magick. Some of these require the channeling of their energy directly into your body and then into the candle (definitely not recommended unless you are familiar with the Deity and its system of magick). Other methods include prayers, petitions, requests, invocations, and rituals. The main object is to imbue the candle with their energy.

Using foreign energy has its advantages in Specialty Candle Magick. It permits you to draw in a singular type of energy that might otherwise be difficult to create. And, just as with using the Earth or Universal energies, you put no unhealthy drain on your own reserves.

The main drawback to the use of foreign energy is that you will need an altar and dedicated room to safely burn more than one candle and perform the magickal act. A circle and dedicated room are necessary to safely call in the Deity. You should never invoke a foreign Deity without having a thorough knowledge of that Deity and the magickal system from which it is derived.

Always call and banish a Deity in the prescribed manner indicated by the system from which it was derived. This is very important even if you are creating your own system of Candle Magick. This will require a lot of homework on your part and should not be attempted unless you are thoroughly versed in the ways of speciality magick. One of our next workbooks will deal with some of the aspects of Speciality Candle Magick, which will include the invocation, banishment and channeling of Deities.

3

Common Oils

Here is a list of commonly used magickal oils. The majority are considered generic and are normally not assigned an astrological ruler, but can be at your discretion. We have placed them under titles indicating their most common usage. Their use may or may not be limited to the category assigned.

SPIRITUAL OR HOLY OILS

ACACIA OIL: Used in rituals for anointing altars, altar candles, and altar cloths. It is used to purify the area.

ALL SAINTS OIL: A generic oil for use with Saints, Loas, and Angels. It brings success to one's endeavors by raising vibrations while rendering protection.

We like to use this oil with a seven-day candle called the Seven African Powers. The candle has seven colors, each attributed to a day of the week. When a candle is burnt on a waxing Moon, the practitioner receives beneficial protection and energy from each of the Saints, Loas, or Weekday Rulers, depending on which system was invoked.

ANOINTING OIL: This is similar to the All Saints Oil and frequently consists of higher vibrational resins and woods, and is used to contact spirits of the higher realms.

BLESSING OIL: An oil for invoking deities in general, it can be used on candles, altars, clothes, and your person.

FRANKINCENSE OIL: This is one of the oldest and most revered oils of all and one of the highest vibrations available today. It is used extensively for protection, purification, and High Magick.

HI-ALTAR OIL: Used for general blessing and consecrating.

INVOCATION OIL: An oil that is used to call the Voodoo Gods. Whenever working with the Loas, always use this oil.

MYRRH OIL: Another of the oldest oils with the highest

vibrations available. A favorite for centuries, it is used mainly for healing, luck, love, money, and hex-breaking.

SANDLEWOOD OIL: See Myrrh Oil.

HAPPINESS AND PROTECTION

APPLE BLOSSOM OIL: Considered a gift of the Goddess, this fragrance uplifts the auric vibration. It is good to ease depression and mood swings in teenage girls.

GERANIUM OIL: An oil of a higher vibration that attracts higher vibrational spirits for mediumship.

LAVENDER OIL: A Goddess oil that raises the vibrations in the home and brings peace. Combine Lavender Oil with Rose Oil and sea salt, place in a spray bottle, and on a waning Moon, spray the corners of the house while visualizing all destructive energies leaving. Burn a lavender candle to finish the cleansing.

LILAC OIL: An oil used in mediumship to bring good spirits and raise the overall vibrations of the house.

LILY OIL: Use as you would Lavender oil.

LOTUS OIL: Use for mediatation or as you would Lavender oil.

ROSE OIL: An essential oil that is used for the protection of women and children. It is the oil of the Great Mother Goddess. Good for protection in magick, particularly when dealing with the elemental kingdoms.

WISTERIA OIL: A very high vibrational oil that is used in ceremonial magick to bring beneficial spirits into the house.

LOVE

ADAM AND EVE OIL: An oil used in love magick by, and for, either sex. Use to anoint a Cherry Red candle for good sexual relations. Burn on Friday.

ARABIAN NIGHTS OIL: An oil for romance, love, and mystery, it is ideal to place on a Cherry Red Adam or Eve Candle (candles that have a human shape) that represents yourself. Burn a little each night and envision the person that you wish to be and how you want others to respond to you.

CAT TAIL OIL: Derived from the plant of the same name and used, primarily by men, to help a lover, usually a woman but not necessarily so, enjoy sexual relations more. Anoint a Cherry Red Adam or Eve Candle. Concentrate on the lovemaking to come while visualizing the reaction you desire from your partner. This oil and candle combination used for the foregoing purpose works exceptionally well when the partner is involved in the magick.

CLEOPATRA OIL: An oil used to make one more attractive to a mate and to spice up the sexual part of the relationship.

FLAMES OF DESIRE OIL: Used to renew or kindle passion in a lover.

GLOW OF ATTRACTION OIL: Mainly used for love magick.

JUNGLE GARDENIA OIL: This is one of the best protective fragrances for women. Being ruled by the Moon, a Pearlesque candle lit on a waxing phase brings protection and the wisdom of women's mysteries.

Worn daily, Jungle Gardenia makes a woman irresistible yet aloof and mysterious. This is a secret passed down to Kala from her mother. If you want to entrance that certain man, wear Jungle Gardenia, the real thing, not a cosmetic synthetic.

LOVE BREAKER OIL: This oil is used to break up a love affair or to send away an unwanted lover.

LYANG LYANG OIL: Used to make one irresistible to others.

MARRIAGE OIL: Used to heal any troubled marriage and help keep it strong. Burn a Red Adam and Eve Candle on Friday during a waxing Moon. What do you think would happen if you burnt this on a waning Moon?

ORRIS OIL: An ancient love drawing oil.

PACHOULI OIL: A love oil used by both male and female for attracting love from either sex.

POWER OILS

ALL SPICE OIL: A hot and fiery oil that gives energy and power. It is often used in place of All Saints Oil in a pinch. All Spice helps to overcome laziness. Use it with an Orange candle on Sunday during the Hour of Mars to motivate.

CINNAMON OIL: Also a hot and fiery oil used for power and energy. It is under the rulership of the Sun, and frequently used in incense due to its unique fragrance. It has been a favorite since ancient times.

SAINT MICHAEL OIL: This oil brings strength and power, and is extremely magnetic. Use on Tuesdays or Sundays during a waxing Moon to win battles, games, and conflicts at work. It is the oil of the warrior.

SAN CAPRIANO OIL: Ideal for winning lawsuits and bringing back an unfaithful lover.

HEALING

HEALING OIL: Effective when used on wax dolls in health magick, it also can be diluted and sprayed around living quarters to banish illness and promote healing.

MAGNET OIL: An oil to heal and draw in energy. It can be used in any magick ritual to attract more energy.

RUE OIL: Especially good for healing and protection, it is a magickal herb oil that will break hexes and restore good health and happiness.

OCCULT STUDIES

DIVINATION OIL: May be used in any form of divination prior to and while you are divining.

SPIRIT GUIDE OIL: Use this oil to call your Spirit Guides while performing magick or engaging in meditation or divination.

WALL BREAKER OIL: An excellent oil to help open up psychic abilities and tear down psychic blocks. It also brings in beneficial energies and prosperity to one's life.

GAMBLING/MONEY OILS

ANISE OIL: An oil for general good luck while gambling.

CARNATION OIL: A hot and fiery oil, under the rulership of Mars. It is used for sexual appeal and gambling by women and men, and brings luck, money, protection, and increased energy.

HAS NO HANNA OIL: This oil is used especially for gambling and, as with many of the gambling oils, is rubbed into the hands prior to gambling. It is also an excellent candle anointment. Burn a twelve-day Orange candle, starting on the New Moon. A picture of the casino, racetrack, etc., is placed before the candle along with a realistic monetary amount one might expect to win. Any remnants of the candle are then placed into a small bag and worn as a talisman around the neck.

FAST LUCK/FAST MONEY OIL: Use this oil with a Green candle on Friday during a waxing Moon.

LOADSTONE OIL: This oil magnetizes all who wear it and all it is placed on. Used on a candle, it draws power into your magick. Attracts money.

THREE JACKS AND A QUEEN OIL: What can we say about this oil that isn't implied in the name? A good oil for luck in card games. Use as indicated in Has No Hanna oil.

VAN VAN OIL: A good oil for luck and power.

ATTRACTION OILS

ATTRACTION OIL: A generic oil that attracts positive vibrations to you and your home. Use on a Monday with a pearlesque candle for protection. Use on Sunday with an Orange candle for happiness, health, and wealth.

BAYBERRY OIL: If this oil is placed on a Green or bayberry candle, it attracts money and good fortune. Burn this combination on a Friday during a waxing Moon, or anoint a twelve-day Orange candle and burn on a Sunday.

BERGMONT OIL: This oil is rubbed into purple candles by practitioners of voodoo to manifest their desires. It can also be used for protection and to manifest money, power and wealth. A very powerful oil, and not for the novice.

UNCROSSING, JINXING, AND EXORCISM

BLACK CAT OIL: An uncrossing oil when rubbed onto a Pink Cat Candle and burnt on a Friday during a waning Moon. A Black Cat Candle burnt on a Saturday during a waning Moon stops gossip. A Green Cat Candle burnt on a waxing Moon restores health to a sick pet. This oil can also be used for hexing and jinxing.

CAT FOOT OIL: From the plant of the same name, this oil is used to divine who is working magick against you. Anoint a twelve-day Yellow candle with this oil, and burn it on a Tuesday until it goes out. During the twelve days, use a method of divination to get your answer or wait and it will be revealed to you.

CIPRIANO OIL: Using this oil will have someone return what is yours, or enable you to find what is lost. This is usually a twenty-one-day Candle Magick rite, utilizing Purple candles.

COUNTERACTING OIL: A hex-breaker. We burn a seven-day Gray candle which neutralizes all energy. Some use a White candle while others will force the hex back to the sender with a double return action, brought about by using a two-color candle, usually Red and Black.

JINX REMOVING OIL: Use this oil to remove and break a jinxed condition. On Saturday, during a waning Moon, burn a seven-day Black candle to break the jinx and return it to the sender. A Double Action Candle can also be used here or you might try a Run Devil Run Candle. To neutralize the condition without a karmic return, burn a seven-day Gray candle.

JU JU OIL: This oil is believed to have been derived from an African witch doctor's formula. It is used for hex breaking or hex creating.

GO AWAY or GET AWAY OIL: Use this oil to send away undesired influences, neighbors, relations, evil spirits, and vibrations.

KEEP AWAY ENEMIES–HATE SPIRITS OIL: Use this oil on a twelve-day Blue candle on a waning Moon. Start on a Monday. This clears undesirable vibrations and influences within any area. Mix with salt, add Blue coloring, and sprinkle around the yard. Mix this oil with Rose Oil, water, salt, and

Blue coloring and spray the house itself.

HEXING, JINXING, AND MISCHIEF MAKING

BATS BLOOD OIL: Used in destructive magick for hexing and jinxing others. Usually placed on Black candles or dolls.

BATS WING OIL: Use this oil, from the plant of the same name, to protect the home and occupants from lightning, sorcerers, etc. It is also known to bring good luck.

BEND-OVER OIL: An oil used to bend others to your will, and for destructive magick on dolls of various compositions.

CITRONELLA OIL: Besides being a great bug repellent, it is usually good for hexing. Convention says that the person being hexed should walk across a path of the citronella. We have found, however, that this is not necessary in hexing or jinxing. Yellow is the key color here and Wednesday is the best day for using citronella. On a waxing Moon, build your hex; on a waning Moon, remove it.

DRAGON'S BLOOD OIL: This oil is used for breaking the most stubborn of hexes since it is an herb of protection and exorcism.

COMMANDING OIL: An oil used not only to command or bend others to your will, but also to make others leave you alone, with a warning of things to come if they don't. Anoint a twelve-day Yellow candle on a waxing Moon. Order this person to leave you alone or the results you must resort to will be on their head, not yours. Envision this person or these persons in your mind and talk with them. Try to resolve the situation. In case you are unaware, talking to a person by visualization is just as good as talking directly to him or her. Next, burn the twelve-day Yellow candle and command them to leave you alone. This rite should immediately calm the situation. Be sure you are innocent of any wrongdoing with regard to it, though.

COMPELLING OIL: An oil used to make others want to do your will even though it may conflict with their will. Use this in conjunction with other oils such as Confusion Oil, Controlling Oil, and Commanding Oil.

CONFUSION OIL: This is used to confuse any issue or

enemy, when you are in a tight spot and need time to think. It buys you time and will cloud the issue. In matters of the law, use this oil on a Purple candle on Thursday. In matters of love, use a Pink candle on a Friday.

CONTROLLING OIL: Used to control a situation, event or another's will. When a son or daughter is out of control and headed for trouble, for example, use this oil to gain control of the situation. Then use Uncrossing Oil and Confusion Oil on a candle called Run Devil Run. This will remove any destructive influences projected from peers and allows you time to reason with your child.

Thereafter, burn a twelve-day Orange candle on Sunday and on a waxing Moon, to build wisdom and strength in the child. Anoint the candle with Frankenscence, Myrrh, Sandlewood, and Cinnamon.

CONQUERING OIL: This oil is used to overpower a situation, conquer paranoias, phobias, and disease. Also use it in conjunction with other oils to ensure success.

CROSSING OIL: This is a hexing or jinxing oil, the reverse of Uncrossing Oil. It is used on dolls and candles for ''Crossing One's Enemies.''

DEVIL'S OIL: This oil, used mainly for hexing and dehexing, puts a block into the path of an enemy. A picture or lock of hair, fingernail clippings, or the like, placed on an altar in front of a dedicated and anointed figure candle, is normally used.

DOUBLE CROSS OIL: Use this oil in conjunction with Confusion Oil, Black Cross, or seven-day candles for confusing, jinxing, or hexing your enemies.

JOB BREAKER OIL: Used to remove an undesirable coworker. Anoint and burn a candle representing the target individual. Obtain a piece of clothing, cigarette, or anything containing the person's essence, which must be rubbed into the candle.

Example: Imbue the candle with the thought of the person and the action to be taken. Anoint with the Job Breaker Oil and the essence. Use another candle to represent the boss (picture attached works best) and anoint this candle with Commanding Oil, Bend-Over Oil, or something similar. Imbue your candle with your will and the action you would like to see taken. Burn both candles for nine minutes each day. Be especially aware of the language of the candle.

You will know that your magick is a success when the flame of the bosses candle rises angrily above that of the target employee. The employee candle should burn twice as fast as the employer candle. The dancing of these flames frequently indicates thoughts, actions or conversations between the two people.

ZODIAC OILS

ZODIAC OIL: This is an oil used for representing the energies of others when you anoint candles, but it can also represent yourself. Zodiac oils help the practitioner to make contact with the ruling elements of each particular house, and are especially good for working on problems that a particular house rules.

4

Examples of Advanced Candle Magick

HEALING GUIDELINES FOR THE ADVANCED MAGICKIAN

At some point in your magickal life, you will want to perform Healing Candle Magick. We have provided two examples for you to consider. The first is for the healing of a person; the second for the healing of an animal. As with all Candle Magick, pick out the parts that work for you and modify the rest.

HEALING A HUMAN BEING

Before you begin any healing of someone else, always ask his or her permission either verbally or by contacting that person's Higher Self. Discuss the situation. The Higher Self may have other plans or the person may not want your interference with the natural course of his or her life. In that case, no amount of medicine or magick will override this decision.

If the person or Higher Self grants you permission, prepare yourself and your equipment as you would in any magickal act.

In order to choose the proper candle or candles for the healing, here are a few suggestions. You can choose a Zodiac Candle if you know the person's birth date. If you do not know it and his or her personality fits that of a certain sign, use a candle of your own choice. You could also use an image candle or a plain candle. Use whatever is appropriate for you and the person. Merge consciousness with the candle and find out what is best to use.

When considering the Moon phase, remember: A waning Moon destroys any disease found in the Aura or body. A waxing Moon builds new health and allows the body to fight the disease. You must decide which tactic works best to heal the person.

Colors must also be carefully chosen and coordinated with the Moon phase as the wrong color during the wrong phase can be trouble. Here are some health associations for several colors in addition to those listed earlier in the book.

COLORS USED FOR HEALING

BLUE: For agitation, allergies, anger, burns, fever, headache, lymph nodes, hot temper, nerves.

GREEN: For balancing, calming, heart problems, hurt feelings, tissue strengthening.

ORANGE: For an antidepressant, bowels, circulation,

energizing, growth, respiratory system, stomach.

PURPLE: For cuts, disinfectant, earaches, eyesight, germicide, sore throats.

RED: For blood building, endurance, heightened senses, increased sex drive, stimulation, strength.

YELLOW: For allergies, bone building, confidence, indecision, liver, memory, mental clarity, wisdom.

HEALING A SICK ANIMAL

Begin by creating a candle that represents the animal. Then, go to your private place and call to the Higher Self of the animal to discuss the situation and ask for guidance and permission to do a healing.

Next, visualize the animal. Look for any diseases or foreign energies that may be draining it. Do not be afraid to look into the organs and tissues. Later, get an animal medical book and compare your findings to it. As your talents grow, you will be able to accurately diagnose many diseases by visualization. Confirm your finding with the pendulum.

For the animal as well as a human, it is best to start the healing on a waning Moon, although this is not always possible in severe cases. This way you have time to remove that which is destructive before trying to heal and build new energy.

Once the clearing process is completed on a waning Moon, begin to build new health on the waxing Moon. Use a Green candle for this rebuilding, by visualizing the animal or person as healthy, radiant, and encased within a protective and healing auric egg. (It is a good idea to clean your own Aura at the same time you clean theirs. This is particularly true if damaging foreign energies were found to cling to the patient.) Continue this cleaning process many times until you can easily visualize a healthy aura about the animal or person.

Call on the patient's Higher Self if you have difficulty. You will be told what more needs to be done, if anything. You will also be told when and if you must release the patient for rebirth along with how to contact the patient again. As difficult as it may be for you, do not argue if and when it is the patient's time to go. You will be doing grave damage to both the patient and yourself. Refer to Rebirthing Guidelines.

5

Rebirthing Guidelines

When a loved one departs, it is critical that a candle be lit to guide their path to the other side (Nirvana, Heaven, Summerland, etc.). This also includes all pets, by the way.

Due to the ignorance of most western religions, many spirits become "earthbound" when they pass out of this incarnation. This means that the individual is tied to the earth plane of existence and is unable to cross over to higher planes for rest, recuperation, and rebirth.

Aside from the religious ignorance of some who remain tied to the earth plane because they refused to believe in an afterlife or reincarnation, many people as well as pets are stranded due to the pull of grieving relatives, loved ones, or friends who refuse to let go. Some are also killed immediately in accidents and do not realize their body is dead. Whatever the reason, a doorway must be created to the other side.

To create the doorway, obtain a minimum three-day candle or, better yet, a seven- or twelve-day Blue or White candle. Dedicate and energize the candle as follows:

Anoint the candle with Sandlewood or Myrrh oil and bring in the Earth and Universal Energies.

Call to the Guardians of Light, or your religious equivalent, to create a path and stairway for the departed.

See a brilliant white stairwell extending upward from the candle into the Astral. You may even see other beings on the stairwell waiting.

Now call to the departed. Do not be surprised if others come as well and follow the deceased up the Astral Stairs. As there are so few who have this knowledge, it is sometimes necessary for the Guardians of Light to bring others who are otherwise stranded or lost.

Deny no one entry; that is not your place. Disregard how they look and allow all who come to cross over. Should someone become obnoxious, call to the Guardians of Light and they will assist this being. You can also tell the being to look around as there are friends and relatives awaiting them.

Frequently, the lost ones cannot see that there are relatives or friends waiting. By your pointing out this fact and their wondering if you are telling the truth, their consciousness clears and allows them to see. Above all, be patient. One of these individuals could have been someone you loved. It might even once have been you.

For pets, see them guided by a divine being representing their species. This is usually a Power Animal or a combination personage such as Bast who will come for cats.

The pet or animal stairwell usually leads directly to what can only be described as a Summer Land. It represents the dream of perfection to all animals, and most humans.

Conclusion

The information and material presented in this workbook will help you along your road of spiritual progression. We have provided the basic mechanics of Candle Magick along with the tools to develop as complicated a system as you may wish. What you develop depends entirely on how much effort you wish to expend.

We firmly believe that our method of Candle Magick will help you not only to create your own Magickal Path, but to expand your awareness to the Universe around you. With this new awareness, you will find your life has a richer and deeper meaning.

Remember, just as each individual is different so is each individual path to enlightenment. Be patient with yourself and others that have not yet discovered this fact.

Kala and Ketz Pajeon

Recommended Books, Videos, and Tapes

BOOKS

African Based Magick
Divine Horseman, by Maya Deren (anthropological). McPherson and Company, 1953.
Santeria, by Migene Gonzalez-Whippler.* Original Products, 3rd ed., 1987.
Chakra Meditations
Opening Up to Your Psychic Self, by Petey Stevens. Nevertheless Press, 1983.
Dictionaries and References
The Donning International Encyclopedic Psychic Dictionary, by June G. Bletzer, Ph.D. Donning Company Publishers, 2d ed., 1987.
The Woman's Encyclopedia of Myths and Secrets, by Barbara Walker. Harper and Row, 1983.
Meditation (Introduction to)
Voluntary Controls, by Jack Schwartz. E.P. Dutton, 1978.
Shamanism
The Way of the Shaman, by Michael Hamar. Bantam Books, 5th printing, 1986.
Basics of Magic, by The Church of the Seven Arrows.* 4385 Hoyt St. #201, Wheaton, Col., 80033.
Secrets of Shamanism, by Jose Stevens, Ph.D., and Lena S. Stevens. Avon Books, 1988.
Ritual Magick
Initiation into Hermetics, by Franz Bardon.* Dieter Ruggeberg, 4th ed., 1981.
Ritual Magick, by Delores Ashcroft-Norwicki.* Aquarian Press, 1986.
Inner Source, by Kathleen Vande Kieft. Ballantine Books, 1988.
Wicce/Wicca
In the Name of the Devil, by Ronald Seth. Tower Publications, 1969.

When God Was a Woman, by Merlin Stone. Harcourt Brace Jovanovich, 1976.

The Holy Book of Women's Mysteries, by Zsuzanna Budapest.* Susan B. Anthony Coven, P.O. Box 11363, Oakland, Calif., 1986.

The Grandmother of Time, by Zsuzanna Budapest. Harper and Row, 1990.

Wicca a Guide for the Singular Practitioner, by Scott Cunningham.* Llewellyn Publications, 1988.

Complete Book of Witch Craft, by Ray Buckland.* Llewellyn Publications, 1986.

Power of the Witch, by Laurie Cabot with Tom Cowan. Delacorte Press, 1989.

* Excellent authors that have written a series of books well worth investigating.

VIDEOS

"Richard Hittleman's Yoga Video Course" (One and Two), by Richard Hittleman. P.O. Box 66640, Scotts Valley, Calif., 95066

"Shirley MacLaine's Inner Workout," by Shirley MacLaine. Vestron Video, P.O. Box 10382, Stamford, Conn. 06901

TAPES

"Creative Visualization," by Shakti Gawain. Whatever Publishing, 158 East Blithedale, Mill Valley, Calif. 94941

"Chakra Meditation," by Potentials Unlimited. 9390 Whitneyville Road, Dept. DS, Alto, Mich. 49302

Bibliography

Aima. *Perfume Oils, Candles, Seals, and Incense.* 4th ed. Foibles Publications, Eldon Publications, 1981.

Bletzer, June, Ph.D. *Encyclopedic Psychic Dictionary.* 2d ed. Norfolk, Va.: Donning Company Publishers, 1987.

Catholic Encyclopedia. Vol. 6. New York: Universal Knowledge Foundation, 1909.

Cirlot, J.E. *A Dictionary of Symbols.* London: Routledge and Kegan Paul, 1962.

Cooper, J.C. *An illustrated Encyclopedia of Traditional Symbols.* New York: Thames and Hudson, 1978.

Culpeper, Nicholas, M.D. *Culpeper's Color Herbal.* New York: Sterling Publishing, 1983.

Cunningham, Scott. *The Complete Book of Incense Oil, and Brews.* St. Paul, Minn.: Llewellyn Publications, 1989.

_____. *The Magic of Incense, Oils, and Brews.* St. Paul, Minn.: Llewellyn Publications, 1986.

Dey, Charmaine. *The Magic Candle.* Bronx, N.Y.: Original Publications, a Division of Jamil Product Corporation, 1982.

Dunwich, Gerina. *The Magick of Candle Burning.* New York: Citadel Press, 1989.

_____. *Candlelight Spells.* New York: Citadel Press, 1988.

Encyclopedia of Religion. Vol. 5. New York: Macmillan, 1987.

Folklore of American Holidays. Detroit: Gale Research Company, 1987.

Gamache, Henri. *The Master Book of Candle Burning or How to Burn Candles for Every Purpose.* Bronx, N.Y.: Original Publications, a Division of Jamil Products Corporation, 1984.

Green, Paula. *Praying With Fire, Candle and Fire Magic.* (self-published.) 1985.

The Jewish Encyclopedia. Vol. 5. New York: Funk and Wagnall's, 1903.

Lampe, H. *Famous Voodoo Rituals and Spells.* Minneapolis: Marlar Publishing, 1974.

Magickal Almanac. St. Paul, Minn.: Llewellyn Publications, 1989.

Oribello, William Alexander. *Candle Burning Magic With the Psalms.* New Brunswick, N.J.: Inner Light Publications, 1988.

Protheroe, W. M., Capriotti, E. R., and Newsom, G. H. *Astronomy.*

Columbus, Ohio: Charles E. Merrill Publishing, 1976.

Riva, Anna. *Candle Burning Magic.* Toluca Lake, Calif.: International Imports, 1980.

_____. *Golden Secrets of Mystic Oils.* Toulca Lake, Calif.: International Imports, 1978.

_____. *Voodoo Handbook of Cult Secrets.* Los Angeles: International Imports, reprint 1989.

Rose, Donna. *Unhexing and Jinx Removing Spells.* Hialeah, Fla.: Mi-World Publishing Company, 1978.

Sharon. *A Basic Guide to the Ancient Art.* (Self-published.) 1984.

Walker, Barbara G. *The Women's Dictionary of Symbols and Sacred Objects.* New York: Harper and Row, 1988.

Wylie, Francis E. *Tides and the Pull of the Moon.* New York: Berkley Books, 1980.

Periodicals and Magazines

Fulghum, Robert. "A Leap for Love." Good Housekeeping, February 1990, p. 172.

Mack, Michael. "Vigil Lights: There's Something Special About the Old Flame." U.S. Catholic, April 1989, p. 29.

Rapp, Joel. "Christmas Legends." Redbook, December 1989, p. 114.

Newspaper Articles

Garcia, Francisco. "Ceremony of Summoning the Departed." *San Jose Mercury News,* The Weekly, October 31, 1990, p. 12.

_____. "Sharing Memories of Loved Ones." *San Jose Mercury News,* Extra 2, October 31, 1990, p. 9.

Kiernan, Vince. "Sun, Moon Cycles Determine When Easter Will Fall Each Year." *The Daily Review,* member of the Alameda Newspaper Group, April 1, 1988.

ABOUT THE AUTHORS

Kala and Ketz Pajeon live in Northern California with their five cats amidst a veritable jungle of herbs. Both are college graduates and conduct research into the various metaphysical philosophies. Combining this research with their writing of both fiction and non-fiction books has been a dream realized for both.

When not writing and doing research into such topics as Hypnotism, Herbalism, Shamanism, Dowsing, Kirlian . Photography, Radionics, Yoga, Akido, and Holistic Healing, their favorite pastime is traveling.

Kala, being descended from a family of Magickal Practitioners, developed her dowsing and channeling skills at an early age. She began Wax Crafting at five, obtained her first Ouija board at nine and her first set of Tarot as twelve. In her early twenties, she rededicated her present lifetime—as she had in previous lifetimes—to her Goddess.

Kala and Ketz have combined Kala's heritage and abilities of channeling the Old and Ancient Ones into a philosophy called Earthcraft. This philosophy emphasises the inner path of each individual and the sacredness of All that is.